THE
FIGHT
FOR
UNION

The Fight

Illustrated

Margaret L. Coit

Houghton Mifflin Company Boston

Books by

MARGARET L. COIT

John C. Calhoun

(*Pulitzer Prize*)

Mr. Baruch

Eighth Printing c

COPYRIGHT © 1961 BY MARGARET L. COIT

ALL RIGHTS RESERVED INCLUDING THE RIGHT

TO REPRODUCE THIS BOOK OR PARTS THEREOF IN ANY FORM

LIBRARY OF CONGRESS CATALOG CARD NUMBER: 61-10634

ISBN: 0-395-06715-4

HOUGHTON MIFFLIN COMPANY BOSTON

PRINTED IN THE U.S.A.

Contents

1   Fire Bell in the Night   1

2   The Missouri Compromise   20

3   The Great Debaters   37

4   The Great Debates   57

5   Tall Tales of Texas   72

6   The Fight for Union   86

7   Wind from the North   104

8   The Powder Keg Explodes   117

    Index   134

List of Illustrations

Following page 24

1. Thomas Jefferson at the age of 78.
2. John Randolph.   A portrait by Harding.
3. Henry Clay at the age of 31.
4. John Quincy Adams.   A portrait by Marchand.

Following page 39

5. Andrew Jackson.   Painting by Chappel.
6. John C. Calhoun.   A portrait by Jarvis.

Following page 64

7. Daniel Webster.   A portrait by Clark.
8. Webster's Reply to Hayne.
9. Sam Houston.   A portrait by Thomas.

Following page 88

10. A photograph of Andrew Jackson in his old age.
11. A photograph of Henry Clay in his later years.
12. John C. Calhoun in his later years.

Following page 104

13. A photograph of Daniel Webster made in 1851.
14. A photograph of Sam Houston in his old age.

Following page 112

15. A photograph of Stephen A. Douglas.
16. A photograph of Abraham Lincoln.
17. The Lincoln Douglas debates.
18. John Brown, painted by N. B. Onthank.

To Those Who
Had Faith

" Our Federal Union: it must be preserved! "

— Andrew Jackson

FIRE
BELL
IN THE
NIGHT

———

1

I‌T WAS 1819. That was the year the fire bell sounded in the night.

Thomas Jefferson heard it even in the bright morning, high on his hilltop at Monticello. Spring was blooming green around him. It was in the smell of the boxwood hedges and the new leaves of the catalpas and the crickets stitching in the locust trees. Looking out, he could see the great walls of blue mountains, and the bright, thin line of the Rivanna River cutting through the green, and the bronze-red road snaking over toward Michie's Tavern, whose whitewashed walls gleamed in the sun. He could see the spires of Charlottesville, three miles away, and the first, faint outlines of that University of Virginia he had dreamed of so long. Almost, it seemed as if he could hear the plop of the earth, as the shovels dug in and the dirt sprayed up while the workmen labored.

All around Mr. Jefferson bloomed the fruition of his dreams: the pink spray of the peach trees marking the boundaries of the four farms he had thrown into one; the beautiful house that he had designed; the state that he had governed; and the young country, which he had seen grow up to take its place among the powers of the world. Now, reality was breaking into those dreams. An ugly sound like "a fire bell in the night" had awakened and filled him with horror.

Missouri had applied for admission to the Federal Union, and the whole ugly question of slavery had broken into debate in Congress. Missouri sought admission as a slave state. But the North was resolved to prevent further spread of slavery, even if the South seceded, even if there was civil war. This was what Mr. Jefferson feared. This was the alarm, the warning that the Union was in danger . . .

Mr. Jefferson had once been a happy man, a man who could make his dreams come true. It has been said that a man's house is his castle, and never was this more true than with Mr. Jefferson's Monticello. It was his own creation, from the time, now fifty years past, when he had sliced off a mountaintop to plant a lawn eight hundred and fifty feet above the valley. Monticello had the first French doors and the first parquet floors, the first storm windows and the first triple window sashes in the United States. The whole house had been designed by Mr. Jefferson himself, as were so many other houses in the neighborhood, for he was an architect. The cool white draperies and blue walls in the dining room, the downstairs guest room in pale green and white with green woodwork and chairs matching the hangings were also designed by Mr. Jefferson, for he was an interior decorator. He was a musician. He was a farmer. He was a philosopher and a practical politician and perhaps the best American prose writer of his day.

Above all, he was that authentic brand of American Yankee — a gadgeteer. He was the most American of men and the most cosmopolitan of Americans. What he liked best was to experiment and invent things.

When he awoke in the morning, it was in a downstairs room, bright with Chinese-red hangings, fringed in gold. No wonder that he usually rose happy to meet the dawn. Mr. Jefferson liked things to be cheerful around him. The bed would swing up to the ceiling on pulleys, and Mr. Jefferson, comfortable in his waistcoat and pantaloons and worn-down bedroom slippers, would pad over to the window, where he could see the wind indicator, looking like a clock, set into the center of the porch roof. He would then look at the barometer and measure the wind.

Then he might step into the hall, where a brass lamp swung gently from an eagle encircled by white marble stars. Against the wall was the beautiful classic statue of the sleeping Ariadne, glimmering white, along with marble busts of Franklin and Patrick Henry, yes, and Alexander Hamilton, too. But Mr. Jefferson's gaze would always move to the big seven-day clock beside the front door, its rows of cannon balls moving down to mark each coming day. Mr. Jefferson had the days spaced apart like the divisions on a ruler, and each was spelled out, there on the wall, except for Sunday. Sunday was in the cellar. Mr. Jefferson liked this clock. He always liked to know where he was in time and space.

On rainy days there was plenty for Mr. Jefferson to do. He could go into the study and twirl around in his red swivel chair, the first swivel chair in the United States. If he was tired, he could stretch out on the red chaise longue, which, of course, was the first American chaise longue.

Being Mr. Jefferson, and full of energy, even in his seventies and eighties, he would more likely be at his desk, precisely listing his flowers and crops in the garden and farm books, or writing down more of his observations on nature and human nature. Now, in these later years, you would be most likely to find him working hard at his desk, drawing, measuring, ruling out the architectural plans for the rotunda, the serpentine walls, the dormitories, the beautiful buildings of the University of Virginia, as we know them today.

But in this sad April of 1819, Mr. Jefferson's mind might have wandered from his routine. He might have mused, somber and silent, at his window, not even seeing the sweep of green hills before him . . . wondering, waiting, for what . . . Then a canter of horses would break the stillness; a visitor would have arrived. Mr. Jefferson would have to shake off his depression and become a gracious host again.

He always did. Although he had been retired from the Presidency now for ten years, he was one of America's first elder statesmen. Everybody who was anybody came to see Mr. Jefferson — counts, princes like the Duke of Saxe-Weimar, or humbly admiring Americans like the dark-eyed, heavy-browed Congressman from Massachusetts, Mr. Daniel Webster.

They saw a man thin and stooping with age, yet with the same swinging walk he had always had, gleams of red still shining in his sandy hair, and in the freckles peppered across his face. He would stroll with his guests across the lawn between the oval and the circular flower beds that he had laid out in 1807. Later, he would call for horses, and the company would ride out across the farm, where every vegetable and fruit and nut that would grow was planted: olive trees, French chestnuts, Italian grapes. And everyone would stop to marvel at the improved plow and threshing machine from Scotland.

There would be tasty home-made bread and fresh vegetables for dinner, and Mr. Jefferson would enjoy it all as much as anyone else. Food came quickly, swinging in on shelves on the revolving doors from the butler's pantry, and the cold drinks would rise from the cellar on the little dumb-waiter elevator. (Mr. Jefferson had invented that, too.)

After coming out of the blue and white Wedgwood dining room, the guests would sit down on the Chippendale chairs in the parlor. There they could smoke and talk and steal glances at the tiny miniature of Tom Paine, which Mr. Jefferson had had especially painted for himself. Or they might play chess, with Mr. Jefferson as the kibitzer, long legs straddling one of his little French Provincial "conversation chairs," and his long chin resting upon the conversational crossbar at the top.

But statesmen were not Mr. Jefferson's favorite visitors. He was the most loving of grandfathers. He always answered his grandchildren's letters. He would give the boys their first riding saddle or their first set of Shakespeare, and a "young lady" her first watch or silk dress.

A tired mother could always leave the children with their grandfather. He would pick fruit for them, stretching his long length to poke down the cherries with a stick. Or he might line the children up for races, with handicaps for the youngsters; count three and drop a white handkerchief. At the end there would be a handful of figs or prunes or dates for the winners.

"I want all my days to end, where all my dreams end, at Monticello," Mr. Jefferson had written. Now his days were ending and his dreams, too. He was awakening from a dream, into the nightmare of reality. It was as though the broad green earth of Monticello had opened, revealing black, quivering quicksand underneath.

Slavery had never been talked about much before. It was being talked about now. It was being debated at every grocery store and crossroads and fireplace and polling place in the United States. Most of all, it was being debated in Congress.

The issue was the Territory of Missouri. Missouri wanted to become a state. It had organized, according to the rules, and applied for admission to the Union. It would be a slave state. Always before, there had been a number of gentlemen's agreements about slavery. If one state came into the Union "slave," the next would come in "free." Now a New York congressman named James Tallmadge moved that if Missouri were admitted to the Union "that the further introduction of slavery . . . be prohibited . . . and that all children born within the said state . . . shall be free at the age of twenty-five years." The debate was on.

What had happened? Slavery had existed in most of the original thirteen states in the Union, but in the North it had gradually died away. As early as 1778, Mr. Jefferson had guided a bill through the

Virginia legislature, stating that no more slaves could be brought into Virginia. By 1808 Congress had outlawed the importation of slaves into the country.

It had always been "understood" that slavery would be ended. The Negroes might be gradually freed, as George Washington had dreamed, or sent back to Africa, so the original "sin" could be righted. This was the hope of Mr. Jefferson. For one thing was certain: it had been almost universally agreed that slavery was a sin. Mr. Jefferson, indeed, feared the terrible vengeance the Negroes might take after three or four generations of outrage. But slavery was not disappearing in the South. Within a few years a new Southern leader, John C. Calhoun, would term slavery "a good, a positive good"; in fact, the most solid foundation for freedom in the world.

What had brought about this terrible change in the hearts of men? Men loved freedom, yes, but they loved making money even more. The new machine, the cotton gin, had made the growing of cotton more and more profitable. Negro slaves were needed all over the South to grow and pick cotton; and where there is a demand, there is a supply. Ships still sailed for the Ivory Coast, some from the

United States and some from other countries. The flag offered protection; no one could stop an American ship at sea. The Negroes were bootlegged, jammed together, shoulder to shoulder and leg to leg, squatting, in holds only three feet deep.

Cotton mills all over the North were calling for tens of millions more pounds of cotton every year. They were calling for farm girls from the hills and immigrants from overseas to work fifteen hours a day, making big profits for the mill-owners.

Yet in the towns in New England, on the little farms, and in the new, half-broken country to the west, more and more voices were raised, louder and louder against slavery. Slavery was nothing to worry about when it was "understood" that it would eventually end. But now it looked as though slavery would stay, and the nation go on — half slave and half free.

The little people in the South were wondering about this question, people who had never owned slaves and never wanted to own them. They were frightened of them. They were frightened because they did not know or understand them. The poor white man would "journey over" to the plantation of a rich man, and look in wonder at what he saw. On one plantation you could see and hear men and women just off the slave ships. Some had the dark and angular features of Arabia and the mental "genius of long-forgotten civilizations." Others, white in their looks, with one eighth or one sixteenth or one thirty-second of Negro blood were still held as slaves.

More and still more Negroes. Always, more and more. Mr. Jefferson said: "I tremble for my country when I remember God is just."

In the four years before the slave trade officially ended, 40,000 "fresh" African Negroes had entered at the port of Charleston alone. Six thousand Negroes a year were leaving Virginia, loading at Alexandria for New Orleans. You heard their feet shuffling, the sound of their chains clanking. Other gangs were moving out from Virginia by way of Kentucky, along the old Wilderness Road and through the Cumberland Gap, where free men had broken the trail. Westward they moved, out into Arkansas and Mississippi and Alabama. Trees, hundreds of years old, were "girdled" and burned to clear the ground, and the free Indians were pushed farther and farther west to make room for Negro slaves.

Slavery was ruining the Old Dominion of Virginia. The land was wearing out; healthy land needed rest and a change in the crops from year to year, not the merciless, one-crop economy of slavery. Those red-glowing fields beyond Monticello were almost as sterile as the fierce sun that burned down upon them. Virginia was becoming useless for tobacco now, but not for the rearing of slaves. Mr. Jefferson had not reckoned with the worn-out tobacco lands or the arrival of the cotton gin. He had not reckoned with the growth of the free population and the slave population. He had not foreseen that the very survival of his beloved Old Dominion might depend on the sales of "likely" colored men and women.

Mr. Jefferson was one of the wisest men the United States have ever produced, yet even he had not seen fully what was going on around him. For everything that he believed was based on his idea of the nature of God and man. He did not agree with the old Puritans that man was born cursed with the original sin of Adam in the Garden of Eden. He believed that man was born good, innocent, in a state of Nature, and that it was only the bad laws men had made that held him down.

The majority of men, Mr. Jefferson said, were "not born with saddles on their backs" for "a favored few, booted and spurred, to ride them." He had seen two revolutions, in France and in America. He had seen men rise up in freedom. He believed in progress. He believed that the revolutions had brought about a change in the nature of man; and, that in the end, all men would be free. And then he heard the bell . . .

Others, too, heard that fire bell tolling . . . A great country was widening out beyond the green slopes of Monticello. Sixteen hundred covered wagons had jogged westward along the Pennsylvania Turnpike within a single year. Only a few years before, the Great Plains had been empty but for Indians and buffalo and the men who hunted the buffalo. Now it seemed as though the whole population was moving westward: Puritans and River Brethren and Scots-Irish, runaway indentured boys and girls, who had been "plucked off the streets of London" and "shanghaied to America," ex-convicts and Southern planters, leaving the drained cotton and tobacco lands behind them, pouring out into the rich new lands ahead . . .

The past was dying, and the men who had hammered out the past. New leaders were growing up who would solve the terrible problems that Mr. Jefferson had left unsolved. Over on Little Pigeon Creek in the Buckhorn Valley of Indiana, where the few settlers were scattered, three to a lonely mile, eleven-year-old Abraham Lincoln played among the beech trees, the elms, and the maples. He strained his young muscles in spring plowing. He bent his young back in fall fodder picking. He turned and twisted his young mind, as over and over he thought of the things he had learned from people who had taught him all that they could teach him.

And the fire bell went on tolling . . .

Thomas Jefferson's cousin heard the sound. John Randolph of Roanoke, as they called him, was almost a skeleton, with long, spindly legs and a whirling forefinger, white and sharp as a bone. In 1819 he was forty-six, but from a distance he still looked like a young boy, and close up, with his wrinkled, withered face, like a very old man. Beneath his funny little visored cap, his eyes glowed black and burning, like those of his Indian ancestor, Pocahontas.

Was he sane or insane? Nobody knew for sure. Once he wrote a letter to a friend. He said that the night before, he had had a personal visit from "His Satanic Majesty," the Devil, who had sat right down at the opposite end of the fireplace from him.

Sometimes Randolph would walk into the House of Representatives in his riding boots, dragging his spurs, with a big hunting dog slinking at his feet. Sometimes he would wear six or eight overcoats, one on top of the other, and before speaking would peel them off and throw them in a pile on the floor.

One thing was certain. Sane or insane, his mind, sharp as the edge of a tomahawk, cut right through to what was important. He saw the big question in the Missouri debate, the big question that Congress would argue over for the next forty years. It was not clear in the Constitution whether Congress or the people of a territory had the final say on slavery. But John Randolph saw that if Congress took the power and outlawed slavery, whatever the people of Missouri thought, this could be done with every new state that came into the Union. It took two thirds of the states to amend the Constitution. When two thirds of the states were free, they could simply pass an amendment outlawing slavery entirely in the South. What would happen to the slaves then — and to the millions of dollars invested in slave property?

The echo of the fire bell sounded in the cabinet meetings of President James Monroe, last of the old

Revolutionary Virginians to become President. Mr. Monroe was a gentle man and a peace-loving one. He had been elected almost unanimously at the beginning of the Era of Good Feeling, and now the brooding storm troubled him. Even more troubled was his brilliant and learned Secretary of State, John Quincy Adams.

Mr. Adams had grown up with the United States of America. His father, John Adams, was the second President. He had gone to Harvard and had been our Minister at the courts of Russia and England.

But he was still a Puritan of Boston, and the whole question of slavery was, to him, a moral question. It was simply a matter of right and wrong. He saw Missouri as "a title page to a great tragic volume." Like the Southern Jefferson, the Northern Adams was trembling for his country. He had no answers. The man with the answers was a tall man from Kentucky named Henry Clay.

Mr. Clay always had answers. For Mr. Clay was a politician, perhaps the most talented politician this country has ever known. Politics, he knew, was the art of making the government work.

All laws, Mr. Clay believed, came about only because men would give in, on both sides. They had to give in a little, if they were to save their country. This was good politics, but it was also patriotism. Mr. Clay was a politician, but he was first a patriot. His country came *first* with him, and the people loved him for it. It was said that if women could vote, he would have been elected hands down.

Not that he was good-looking, really; he had masculinity, swagger, charm. He had a long mouth, curling up at the corners, and shapely legs and a jaunty tilt to his shoulders. He was cocky and impudent, and even when old, he seemed very young. He had been the youngest senator in our history. But soon he had moved over to the House, because more important matters were going on there. And ever since the smiling "cock of Kentucky" had arrived to take his seat in the House of Representatives, he had been the most important man in Congress.

He took his duties as Speaker literally. When he wanted to speak (which was often) he stepped down from the chair and spoke. He was not a profound man. He was a self-educated, poor country boy from the worn-out "slashes" section of Virginia, who had moved on to Kentucky and seen there the promise of the new West, in the deep blue grass, the lush tobacco fields, the beautiful horses. Loving Kentucky, he came to love all the more the United States of America.

Now, with the fire bell sounding, his thoughts were dark with foreboding, as he listened to the clamor about him. He sat, long and lounging and graceful, in his chair in the House. His hand rested firmly on the gavel. Now and then his bright gray eyes circled the chamber, moving upward along the line of the tall marble columns. It was a beautiful room. And America was a beautiful country . . .

Now, it was not of a peaceful, united country that men talked. They feared that if Missouri set up her own government outside the Union, the North would try to bring her in by force. If so, the South would fight. "Do you believe," shouted John Tyler of Virginia, "that Northern bayonets will ever be plunged into Southern hearts?"

Visitors in the gallery noticed that Henry Clay looked pale and tired. He was very tired. It was a strain just keeping order amidst such wild emotion. The air, heated by stoves, was close and warm and stale. Furthermore, Clay had been calling night sessions, in an effort to wear the speakers out.

And he shrank from what he heard. His own

father had died during the Revolution. He could
remember his horror when, as a little boy of four,
he had seen British soldiers, seeking treasure, ram
their bayonets into the newly dug grave. Perhaps
his hatred of war and also his patriotism had been
born then — all he knew was that he could stand
no more of this now. Perhaps the South was bluff-
ing; he only hoped that it was. "I never despair of
the Republic," he said. He knew that he himself
must speak soon for "poor, unheard Missouri." He
drew away from the hot breath of the candles on
his cheek, then wearily brought his gavel down.
And tired men kept on shouting to be heard over
each other, as the "Misery Debates" wore on.

THE
MISSOURI
COMPROMISE

2

HIGH POINTS in the life of
Henry Clay seemed always to come in the sleet and
the rain. Sleet was clicking against the skylights on
the February afternoon in 1820 when the Missouri
debates rose to a climax as heated as the sodden ice
outside was cold.

All the ugly feelings, glossed over by years of
"understanding," and of looking the other way, had
risen to the surface. The bitter words "disunion"
and "civil war" cut across the tense room. Henry
Clay could not bear to hear them. Nothing would
be worse than a civil war. A free and united
America was the hope of the world. All over South
America, newborn republics were looking to the
United States for hope and inspiration. The Union
must hold firm. The question of slavery was noth-

ing compared to the preservation of the Union itself.

Clay arose and looked around the House Chamber. Since noon, the galleries and floor had been filling. He knew what people were saying about him. He was "the great Mr. Clay," the very "soul of the House of Representatives." He must not disappoint them.

Negro slaves were there. Ladies were there, hundreds of them, crammed on sofas along the walls, sitting in great circles of ruffles and billows upon the stone steps leading up to the galleries. They had even pushed the congressmen out of their own seats. They were giggling and whispering and passing little oranges and cakes to each other. You could scarcely hear the men. But you could hear the shrill voice of John Randolph of Roanoke.

"Mr. Speaker!"

Clay started. It was as though the eyes of John Randolph were drilling right through him. He nodded his head.

"Mr. Speaker!" Randolph's voice shrilled to a higher pitch. He shook his bony, white finger. "What are all these women doing here? They had much better be at home attending to their knitting."

Probably Clay agreed. He tried to look stern.

But the corners of his mouth were twitching. Around him, men were smiling and chuckling, all but two. They were standing against the wall. It is doubtful if Clay even saw these two United States senators, Jesse B. Thomas, of Illinois, and Jonathan Roberts, of Pennsylvania.

"Randolph is mad," Thomas said.

"But dangerous," Roberts added. "He is the most rabid of all the Southerners." Randolph would work openly for secession, if Missouri were denied statehood. And he had a great deal of influence, especially among the Virginians.

The two visitors waited to hear what Henry Clay had to say. It turned out that he had no particular plan. He took the Southern side of the question, although with no threats, no talk of secession. What he talked about was Missouri. Alabama, Mississippi, Louisiana, Tennessee, his own Kentucky. All had come into the Union with no restrictions as to slavery. Why not Missouri?

Not that he was in favor of slavery, Clay added. If he were a citizen of Missouri, he would hope that no more slaves would be brought in. He was not a citizen of Missouri, and slavery was not the question. The point was that Missouri had every right to come into the Union, as the other states had come, without restrictions, either as to slavery or to freedom.

For four hours he held that big hall silent. All were watching the play of emotion on his sensitive face, the long, graceful gestures of his hands and arms and swaying body. His voice was like music. Slowly, darkness filled the windows. Candles blazed up in the chandelier; the voice died away, and Henry Clay was swallowed up by the crowd.

The two senators detached themselves from the wall, and fought their way through the people. They reached the Speaker at last.

"A fine speech, Mr. Clay," Thomas said.

Henry Clay thanked him. He knew it was a fine speech.

"May we have a word with you?"

Now, Clay really looked at them. This was important. "Certainly," he said; and together they battled their way out to the corridor.

The two senators spoke a word. It was *compromise*. Henry Clay bridled. "We have no need to compromise," he said. "Missouri's cause is as good as won."

The senators did not agree. "I'm afraid you're underestimating the determination of the Northerners," Thomas said. "Or the threats of the South

. . . the South will secede if we cannot reach a compromise."

At that, Henry Clay just threw back his head and laughed. The senators saw that it was no use to talk to him. He brushed them off, lightly. "You are taking . . . my Southern friends a little too seriously," he said.

"If you change your mind, Mr. Clay," Thomas persisted, "you can find me at my lodgings."

But Clay was very tired, and he had had enough. "Good night, gentlemen," he said, and put on his coat and hat. Halfway down the corridor, he looked back: "I'm going to Kentucky," he shouted, jokingly, "to raise troops to defend Missouri."

Someone stirred in the shadows, a lean figure, long and silent-moving, like an Indian. "Mr. Clay," he called. The Kentuckian turned.

"Mr. Clay," the strange, high voice of Randolph of Roanoke sounded: "I will follow you to Kentucky, or anywhere else."

John Randolph's eyes were glittering under the long-visored cap he wore. Hastily, Clay invited him into his office. Candles were lighted. The two men sat down opposite each other at a table.

Randolph burrowed deep into his pockets. Up

1 Thomas Jefferson at the age of 78.
   Detail from a painting by Thomas Sully

2 John Randolph.
   A portrait by Chester Harding

3 Henry Clay at the
age of 31.
*A miniature
painted by
Maldemant Mentelle*

4 John Quincy Adams.
A portrait by Edward D. Marchand

came a package of papers, which he flung before
Clay.

"These are our plans," he said. "We intend to
call a convention to vote on secession. Read the
signatures . . . You will find . . . many of your
friends."

Grimly, Henry Clay read on and on. So those
two Northern senators had been right after all.
John Randolph broke into his musings. The South
would defend Missouri by the sword, Randolph was
saying. "Are you ready to buckle on your armor,
Mr. Speaker?"

Clay played for time. "I cannot take so serious a
step without thinking it over," he said.

"Until tomorrow then." Suddenly, the papers
were gone. John Randolph was gone. Henry Clay
was alone in the room.

He must have air. He stumbled to a window and
jerked it open. Below him lay the city of Washington, wrapped in the peace of night and new-fallen
snow. Against the white, he saw the dark lines of
the poplar trees, the trees that Thomas Jefferson
had planted. If civil war came, Washington would
be a battleground once more, as in 1812, . . . again
the White House on fire . . . the silent bodies in the

battlefields. Clay knotted his fists together. What had those Northern senators said? Compromise . . . if you change your mind . . . bring North and South together . . . compromise.

Within five minutes, Henry Clay was fumbling his way through the dark streets and snow toward the lodgings of Senator Thomas.

Spring had come to Washington. It was in the green melting over the trees and the yellow fountains of forsythia. It was in the shouts of the children, released from the stuffy houses and heavy clothes of the wintertime. The sun shone.

In the Congress of the United States the great storm of debate still raged. But the question was coming to a vote. The sides were lining up for a count. The Missouri question was about to be settled, and with it perhaps, the fate of the Republic, the issue of peace or war.

The details of the proposed Missouri Compromise were now before the public. It worked this way: Missouri was to enter the Union the way it wished, as a slave state. This would please the Southern slaveholders. But an imaginary line was to be drawn westward across the American continent, straight from Missouri's southern border, and, henceforth no more slavery was ever to be permitted above that line. This was to please the North. Finally, when Missouri came in as a slave state, Maine was to come in as a free state, and thus the balance of power in the Senate would be maintained.

The North really was getting the better of the bargain. For, at that time, the United States did not own much land south of the "compromise line" of Missouri. Most of that big area south and west of Missouri belonged to Mexico; it did not look as if there could be many more slave states. You would have thought the North would have been pleased with the Compromise. But to the North, any extension of slavery was wrong, and you cannot compromise with wrong. So the vote in the House was doubtful.

Henry Clay worked hard to have the Compromise accepted. This is why history would give him the credit for it. He knew you could not argue with principles. He knew that you could not change minds that had already been made up. But he knew how to win people who had not yet made up their minds.

He was six votes short of a majority. He turned his attention toward six men from the North. He flattered them. He charmed them. He passed them his snuffbox. He asked their advice. He even walked home with them in the evenings. Did they not realize, he pointed out, that unless they agreed to restrict slavery somewhere, it might spread everywhere? Was this what the North wanted?

The congressmen could not resist him: his logic, his smile, his charm. The charm had such impact that an important Democrat visiting Washington actually refused to meet Henry Clay. He said that he did not want to be exposed to the power of his fascination.

The three men from New York held out. They would be defeated back home, if they voted for the Compromise. Clay had a solution. Why didn't they just stay away the day the vote was taken? They did stay away. When the vote was called, Henry Clay and the Compromise won — by a margin of three votes. Clay leaned back in relief. Then a familiar voice shrilled across the chamber. John Randolph of Roanoke wanted the floor.

Henry Clay had not won Mr. Randolph. Since that snowy night in the Speaker's office, Randolph had been sure that Clay had deliberately cheated him. He had spent weeks insulting the Speaker from the floor. He had sneered at Mr. Clay's lack

of formal education. He had made fun of the way
he had pronounced words. He had blamed Clay,
the onetime War Hawk, for all the defeats of the
War of 1812, and for all the mistakes in foreign
policy.

Clay had pretended not to hear. He had played
with his snuffbox and rattled the papers on his desk.
Sometimes he had left the chair and paced the floor.
Now he had won, and Randolph's fury was un-
bounded. The Southerners, as a whole, had stopped
talking about disunion. But John Randolph was
still shrewd enough to pull one more trick out of his
hat. He moved for a reconsideration of the vote
just taken on the Compromise.

This was bad. Representatives had already scattered. Others might have to leave the room or
attend committee meetings or go home. Already,
angry Northerners were working on the floor, trying to find the three necessary votes. Suddenly,
lightning flashed through Henry Clay's nimble
mind. He stood up. The motion to reconsider
would not be in order, he told Mr. Randolph, until
the members had disposed of the routine business
of the day.

The House buckled down to work. It was a scene
of buzzing and confusion, bills being brought up,

others being sent out to committee, pageboys running up and down. Clay moved quietly and quickly. He found a pen. He made sure the point was blunt and strong. Then he signed his name and scattered sand across the paper to blot the ink. He handed the paper to the Clerk of the House and asked him to take it over to the Senate. Suddenly, the Clerk grinned . . .

Clay's gavel sounded; the House was again in order. Again, John Randolph put his motion.

"The motion is out of order," Speaker Clay retorted. "The bill . . . has gone to the Senate."

Clay never forgot the look of hatred on John Randolph's face. It all came back to him six years later when Randolph leveled a new attack on him in the Senate, where Clay was not a member and not able to defend himself. There was no need to ask the ladies to leave this time. Sick with disgust, they fled from the chamber. Senator after senator tried to quiet Randolph, but it was impossible. He called Henry Clay a Judas. He called him a blackleg. He said that he was like "a rotten mackerel by moonlight; he shines and stinks."

That night Mr. Clay opened a polished wooden box and ran his hands over the shining barrels of two pistols, nested on a bed of velvet. Then he sat down and sent a letter to Randolph. It was a challenge to a duel.

John Randolph was the most famous duelist of his time. If he could not taunt a man into challenging him, he would send a challenge himself. Daniel Webster of Massachusetts, the most peaceful and reasonable of human beings, gave him his comeuppance. Webster wrote Randolph that his career meant something to him, and he was not going to risk his life to please a madman.

Webster could afford to do this, because New Englanders did not recognize quarrels of "honor." In the South, it was different. If Clay had ignored Randolph's remarks, he would have been branded as a coward. It did not matter that he had only fired a gun two or three times in his life, and that Randolph was one of the best shots in Virginia. It did not matter that Randolph was a bachelor, and that Clay had a houseful of little children. Clay had had enough of hurts and taunts. He determined to kill John Randolph, or be killed. No one could stop him.

As for Randolph . . . His friend Thomas Hart Benton, of Missouri, visited him the night before the duel and found him calm and cool. He had been to the bank to get some gold coins to give his valet, Johnny, in case of his death, and was now sitting quietly, thinking about the uncertain future. Benton appealed to him to remember Henry Clay's wife and children.

"I shall do nothing to injure the children or the mother," Randolph said. Benton wondered what he meant.

The day dawned; the hour of the duel was at hand. Across a space of green, the two men faced each other. Afterward, Henry Clay remembered the smell of the violets that choked the woods, and the look of the doctor's bag, waiting nearby. Randolph was outlandishly dressed, in a kind of white, flowing bathrobe. There was no making out his skeleton figure under that voluminous cover. Clay's heart sank.

Boldly, he lifted his gun and fired straight at John Randolph. The bullet sang through the cloth, but Randolph did not waver. Clay had to wait now. Randolph fired — fired into the ground, then walked slowly toward Clay with his hand outstretched.

"I do not fire at you, Mr. Clay," he said. Anger drained out of Henry Clay; honor had been satisfied. He and Randolph shook hands.

"You owe me a new coat, Mr. Clay," the Senator from Virginia said.

"I'm glad the debt is no greater," replied Henry Clay. He *was* glad. This had not been a very peaceful act on the part of the man who was already called "The Great Pacificator." But much could be forgiven Henry Clay, the man who had for the time being saved the Union.

For he had saved it. Everyone agreed as to that. Henry Clay had done all that one loyal and patriotic man could do. Was it enough? Overhead, the skies were open and clear. But far away on the horizon clouds lingered, and thunder muttered sullenly.

There was still a good deal of discussion in the cabinet meetings of President James Monroe. The members were not satisfied with the settlement. The President wondered, if a law was ever passed forbidding slavery in a territory, would it still apply when that territory became a state? If so, would not the state then be prevented from joining the Union on an equal footing with other states?

Secretary of War John C. Calhoun had an answer. Calhoun was a slender, dark-eyed man, thirty-seven years old, but bent on one purpose. Young though he was, he wanted to be President, and already men were talking about him. He was doing a good job as Secretary of War. Daniel Webster had unofficially endorsed him for the Presidency.

Calhoun was a South Carolinian and a slave-holder, but he wanted to lead a united country. The Missouri Compromise, he thought, had pulled the country together again. The one thing that might bring about disunion, he feared, would be a belief in the slaveholding states that the North somehow intended to cheat the planters out of their slaves. Why worry as to whether the Missouri Compromise would last "forever"? Calhoun asked. Why not just say it was constitutional, and let it go at that?

John C. Calhoun would live to regret his words.

Secretary of State John Quincy Adams, who was destined to be the next President of the United States, was still worried. To him, the Compromise was nothing but a law to continue slavery. "Such a bargain between freedom and slavery," he said, was "morally and politically vicious." He felt that it violated the very principles upon which we had fought the American Revolution. This slavery question was nothing that could be "winked away by a compromise."

Thomas Jefferson at Monticello felt much the same way. Never again would there be peace and happiness for him on those green slopes. The "fire bell in the night" was still sounding, tolling now the death of the Union. This was what Mr. Jefferson heard. The slavery uproar was indeed "hushed . . . for the moment." But Jefferson knew that this was only a reprieve. To reduce a moral principle to a geographical line across a map could only mean dissension and tragedy.

So old Thomas Jefferson, one of the last of the Revolutionary patriots, listened to the storm gathering, a storm that would wreck the Ship of State he had helped launch. But the American people, did not hear. For almost a generation, the sound of the fire bell was stilled. Meanwhile an age was drawing to its close . . .

The fiftieth anniversary of the Republic was at hand, the fiftieth anniversary of the signing of the Declaration of Independence. The year was 1826. Still alive were two of the most beloved of the Founding Fathers, old friends who had quarreled and now were friends again: eighty-three-year-old Thomas Jefferson, of Virginia, and ninety-one-year-old John Adams, of Massachusetts.

Mr. Jefferson had been invited to attend a fiftieth anniversary celebration. He did not think he would be able to go. But he wrote a message, voicing once more his old dream. "All eyes," he wrote, "are opening to the rights of man."

His day had passed. He lay back and let the life drain slowly out of him. It was the third of July. He could not get up to see the wind indicator, or walk out to look at the day-clock in the hall. Body and soul labored together in low ebb in the hours before dawn. If only he could live until the Fourth of July . . .

The morning came, and the noon and the night. Once more, Mr. Jefferson saw the sun lift itself over the mountain slope. It was the Fourth of July, and he died in the afternoon. In far-off, granite-ribbed Massachusetts, John Adams, former President and father of the President of the United States, lay on his bed. Dimly, he could hear the shouted words of the toast he had written: "Independence forever!" And, as his life ebbed away, he spoke once more: "Jefferson still lives," he said.

It was the Fourth of July, 1826, and the United States of America was fifty years old. Far in the distance, the fire bell was echoing . . .

THE
GREAT
DEBATERS

3

O NE THING is certain: in
the 1820's, the great American game was politics.
There are good reasons for this. For one thing, the
so-called Era of Good Feeling was really a time of
very bad feelings indeed. It was a time of big politics, and Americans have never been able to resist
the fun and fights of big politics. From the first
town meetings of rural New England to the national
telecasts of the party conventions, politics has ranked
as the number one American game, perhaps even
more than big-league baseball. So, for fifteen years,
as the black clouds of storm gathered, Americans
played the great American game. It was a time when
our national two-party system was born.

Now, politics is, most of all, people. Never had
the people in American politics been more colorful
than in the 1820's. There was Henry Clay. There

was John Randolph. There was John Calhoun.
There was Daniel Webster. There was John Quincy
Adams, son of old John Adams. And there was
Andrew Jackson.

It was around Andrew Jackson and John Quincy
Adams that the big storms of the 1820's were blow-
ing. Most of the people wanted Andrew Jackson for
President in the election of 1824, but John Quincy
Adams was legally elected. It happened this way:

There had been four candidates in the race, and
although Andrew Jackson had received the highest
popular vote, no man had won a majority of the
electoral vote. So, as the Constitution provided, the
House of Representatives had to choose the President, and in the House a defeated candidate, Henry
Clay, was still the most powerful man. Clay threw
his own votes to John Quincy Adams of Massachusetts, who, he thought, would make a better President than General Jackson. Adams had had more
training for the job.

Now, no one denied Mr. Adams' qualifications.
He was a Harvard man and a President's son, and a
former senator and a former Secretary of State. But
he was also the kind of New England Yankee that
was hard for the rest of the country to understand.
He was not warm and glowing and earthy, like the

self-styled "New Hampshireman," Daniel Webster. He was as hard as granite, as tough as a hickory nut, and as wry as a crab apple.

Character he certainly had, and he had to have a lot of it to stand up under the punishment he was to take for the next four years. Adams was a great man, but he never had a chance to do much as President. Congress was against him. His own party, his own Vice-President, John C. Calhoun, opposed him. Even his fellow aristocrat John Randolph of Roanoke felt that the people had been robbed of their choice. So the full four years of Adams' administration were just one long presidential campaign for Andrew Jackson.

Andrew Jackson, the hero of the Battle of New Orleans, was certainly the wrong man to deprive of the presidential office. For he later became one of the most popular Presidents the United States ever had, and he was the greatest popular hero since George Washington's time. Fifty years and more after his death, in some backwoods parts of the South, people were still voting for Andrew Jackson.

He was a striking-looking man. He was long and lean and rambunctious, with blue eyes that blazed, and his once-red hair reared up like a crown, stiff and white on the top of his head. "King Andrew, the First," his enemies called him. It did not matter. What he stood for politically was never quite clear; but no one really cared too much about that.

As a matter of fact, Jackson had plenty of ideas. He had ideas about big business (he was against it), about labor (he was for it), and, in the end, his Presidency would transform, not only the Democratic party, but the whole meaning of American democracy. His administration marked a turning point. He did not believe, as Jefferson had, simply that all men should have an equal chance. He really believed that all men were equal, and that all could do an equally good job, if given the chance. This was the idea that came out of the Jacksonian Revolution, but nobody realized this at the time.

As one of his biographers, Gerald Johnson, has written: Jackson came roaring into history with a sword cut on his skull. He was a soldier of the Revolution and taken prisoner when he was only a boy of fourteen, and a British officer had slashed his head with a sword, because the boy had refused to polish the Englishman's boots.

He had been a frontier strong-man when Tennessee was the farthest outpost of the Wild West of his day, and when fighting settlers often bit off each

5 Andrew Jackson.
Painting by Alonzo Chappel

6   John C. Calhoun.
    A portrait by John Wesley Jarvis

other's noses and ears. As judge of the brawling
territory, Jackson had enforced order and law at
gunpoint, taming down citizens who had often left
their native areas by official request, or by night,
with undue speed.

He was almost a folk myth when he became President, the symbol perhaps, of the American frontier.
He never cringed; he never backed down; he never
ran away. He hated and loved and strutted in-
cessantly, and the people loved him for it. He did
things that the average man was too timid to try,
but nothing that the average man could not understand. As a soldier, he had won victory both from
primitive Indian tribes and from trained British
officers who had faced Napoleon. He had lived on
acorns and slept in the rain; his body was scarred
with smallpox and bullet wounds. He had had little
education, but he knew a lot about people. Perhaps
that was why the people trusted him. He was cun-
ning and shrewd and "simple as an axe handle."

Andrew Jackson had come to Washington to take
over a country very different from the little Federal
Republic, in which he had served a youthful term as
senator, back in the year of Washington's Farewell
Address. Now, the miracle of the railroads had come
to pass. A company called the Baltimore and Ohio

had laid lines on the earth, reaching toward the horizon, and freight cars moved along them at fifteen miles an hour. In 1829, the year of Jackson's inaugural, Mr. Jefferson's Monticello had been sold for only $2500. Nearly half the population of Virginia had moved away. The land was wearing out; production was falling in the old Cotton States; as early as 1821, a third of the total cotton crop was being raised in states west of the Alleghenies.

The old days and the old ways were changing, and Andrew Jackson was the symbol of the change. "When he comes, he will bring a breeze with him," Daniel Webster, now a senator from Massachusetts, had written. "Which way it will blow, I cannot tell."

Ten thousand people piled into Washington for the inauguration of Andrew Jackson. Some had walked a hundred miles to see their hero. They wore buckskins and moccasins; they tracked the dirt of the Western trails into the White House. In the excitement, they smashed the furniture and china in the reception rooms, and almost squeezed poor Jackson to death against the wall. They climbed up all muddy on the chairs to see him, and whooped and yelled like Indians.

None of this surprised anybody very much. Everyone knew that Jackson was for the plain people, for the New West, as against the ruling classes of New England and the Old South. The people had come to Washington to take over their own government; that was all.

What was surprising was the literary and very statesmanlike tone of the new President's inaugural address. He could not possibly have written it, his enemies said. The General grinned, clamping his teeth down on the stem of a corncob pipe. "Don't I deserve just as much credit for picking out the man who could write it?" he demanded.

What were the issues of the time? To Andrew Jackson, the big danger was the National Bank, where the government kept its funds. It was controlled by business leaders, whom Jackson suspected of using the Bank's money and power to influence the government. But to the majority of Southerners, the big question was the tariff. There is no subject that is more dull than the tariff. But there are few that are more important.

A tariff is a tax on foreign goods coming into a country. If the tax is paid, it raises the price of these imported goods, and has two other results, as well.

First, it discourages the people of the United States
from buying so many things manufactured abroad;
and second, it allows American manufacturers to
charge higher prices for their goods and still sell
them for less than the imported products. A tariff
which does these things is called a "protective tariff."
A tax on foreign imports that is too low to raise their
price any higher than those of products manufactured in the United States is called "a tariff for
revenue." Its purpose is simply to provide extra
money for our government.

There had been tariffs for revenue since the for-
mation of the Union, but as the United States manufactured very few things then, there was no need
for a protective tariff. But when England went to
war, first with France, and then with the United
States between 1812 and 1815, it was hard to get
goods from Europe, and the United States had to
start its own factories. In Boston, Paul Revere made
copper sheathing for "Old Ironsides" and other
American ships of war. Spinning mills were pow-
ered by the falls in Paterson, New Jersey, and later
would come the woolen and cotton mills in the
Merrimack Valley in Massachusetts.

It cost a lot to build mills. The owners had to
recover some of the costs from the price of their

products. Then when the wars were over, Europe began to flood the United States market with cheap manufactured goods. And a protective tariff became a permanent policy of the government.

This was fine for the millowners and the workmen in the North. But the farmers and planters in the South were not pleased. They manufactured very little, and they had to sell their cotton and corn and tobacco in the free markets of the world. In the years of "bumper crops," they got a very low price. They could not afford to pay high prices for their furniture, their clothes, their farm machinery, and other manufactured things. For years, they had bought most of their goods from Europe, which, in turn, bought their farm crops. Now they had to pay more than they could afford for everything but their food, so that the American manufacturer in the North could make a profit. The Southerners were angry.

They knew that the government was piling up money in the Treasury. They did not object to a tariff "for revenue" only, to help finance the government. But did a government, set up for the "general welfare" of all the people, have a right to help one section grow rich, at the expense of the other one growing poor? The Southern farmers were not asking for "federal aid" for themselves. They just wanted the government to stop helping the manufacturers. The South was in revolt. And the leader of this farm revolt was a man from South Carolina named John C. Calhoun.

John C. Calhoun was the first of a long line of statesmen who spoke for the South. He wanted to turn the clock back. He wanted the kind of America that Mr. Jefferson had dreamed about: a peaceful, farming America, unmarked by big cities and big industries. He wanted a population of landowners and homeowners, not men who rented their houses from others and worked for wages paid by other men. The Southerners felt that such people could not call their homes or their jobs or even their very souls their own.

Calhoun knew that the America he loved was going up in the smoke of a thousand new factory chimneys. He did not grudge the workman his right to his job. All he asked was that the life he loved be saved for those who wanted to live and work on the land; farming, he maintained, was not a business, but a way of life.

He, himself, had come out of this way of life. Born during the last year of the Revolution, he had grown up in a farmhouse on the rough, lonely South Carolina frontier. His father was an Irishman from County Donegal, an Indian fighter, and leader of the Border Patrol. Patrick Calhoun could remember the Long Cane Massacre, and the bodies of his mother and brother, killed by Indians; and another brother, who had died during the Battle of Cowpens in the Revolution. He was stubborn and cranky; he had no respect whatever for laws or orders that restricted his own freedom. He had marched down to Charleston from the mountains, to seize the right to vote at the point of a gun. That government was best, he felt, which governed least. It is easy to see why his son, John, would have been against a protective tariff.

Pat Calhoun died when his son John was thirteen. The boy grew up in peace and loneliness — a few months in a log cabin school, learning to spell out his letters and to write his name . . . a few old books in a brother-in-law's library to wonder about and muse over . . . hours of heat and sweat and sun . . . wet weeds tickling his bare feet and ankles . . . the plow handles dragging heavy in his hands.

A thousand miles to the north, young Daniel Webster was struggling with his Greek and Latin and table manners at historic Phillips Academy in

Exeter, New Hampshire. Westward, in Kentucky, Henry Clay was learning the ways of men at the race tracks and dancing assemblies. But Calhoun was studying the depth of the blue shadows streaked along the logs of the corncrib, and the play of color and light over the banks of red clay. Always, he was thinking. Time and years wore on, and the neighbors stopped, startled, to watch the young man plowing in the cotton fields, with a book tied to the plow.

Time began to speed up. Calhoun had wanted to be a farmer, but he became a statesman. Yale University. Litchfield Law School. The South Carolina legislature. The House of Representatives. The War Department and the Vice-Presidency. In 1829, John C. Calhoun was forty-seven years old. He was restless and eager and somewhat worn down by his eagerness. Like Jackson, he was long and lean and a little stooped, and his dark eyes blazed with light when he was excited.

His early dreams seemed far away now. Once he had longed to be President. But he had broken with John Quincy Adams, and had differed with Andrew Jackson. He still hoped to be President, but there were things that he wanted more. He loved the South and the land and the way of life on the land, and the kind of Union in which that way of life could last.

During the summer months of 1827 and 1828, many of the Southern leaders had found their way to Calhoun's home, Fort Hill, a long, narrow, whitewashed dwelling in the blue foothills near Pendleton, South Carolina. Here, for a few months each year, between congressional sessions, Calhoun could turn farmer and live the life he loved. Here, broad, red-clay fields faded into rose, into pink and violet under the shifting light of the sunset, and stark, black pine crowned the ridges of the hills.

Here, Calhoun labored under the sun, as he had when he was a boy. He experimented with plaster of Paris as a fertilizer. He saw that the cotton was planted three feet apart both ways so as to prevent the growth of weeds in the shadows. In the cotton fields, he instructed the "hands" to set the plow diagonally from one curving terrace to another, so that the harsh brown stalks from last year's crop would not scratch the legs of the horses.

In the evening, he might walk down past the fields to the river, where steep little hills sloped into narrow ravines, and through the tangle of brush and branches, the river bed glowed pink below the rush of silvery water. Nothing on earth stirred Calhoun so much as the beauty of this Southern farm country, the flame-tinged sunsets, the fields of bursting cotton or bending grain, the clean wind from the mountains whipping through the rows of cedar trees that curved around the drive. Nothing on earth had such power to give him joy or to bring him peace.

On summer nights Calhoun received guests on the white-columned porch of Fort Hill, the air heavy and dense with the smell of boxwood hedges and tangy with the scent of mimosa. Calhoun would rise to greet his visitors, towering over them in a suit of home-grown nankeen cotton. He would joke about his six feet two inches of height: "George Washington and I," he would say.

They would eat a supper, perhaps, of cottage cheese and cream. The porch would be littered with saddles and children's toys and a forgotten gun or two. A dog's tail might thump, suddenly, or the sound of a guitar strum across the darkness. Into the night, the voices would rise, seeking, searching, and hours after the voices and carriage wheels had died away, Calhoun would be there on the porch, still, his restless footsteps echoing, as he paced and paced and thought and thought, until the darkness paled slowly into dawn.

The result of his thinking was a long paper,

adopted by the South Carolina legislature in the fall of 1828. It had a long title, too: "The South Carolina Exposition and Protest." There was no name signed to this paper, but it slowly leaked out who had written it: Mr. John C. Calhoun, the Vice-President of the United States. "We have taken the ground," he wrote a friend, "that the South is in danger and must be saved."

The "Protest" is difficult to read and to understand, but it does boil down to a few basic ideas. For one thing, it argues that the American *people* did not make their government, but that the *states* created the United States of America. The thirteen states had banded together in an agreement to set up a government. They had drawn up a constitution to set the limits of that government's power. Hence, if a state thought a law was unconstitutional, it could refuse to obey (as Louisiana tried unsuccessfully to do during the school integration crisis of 1960). After all, the Southerners argued, the Constitution itself stated clearly that all powers not granted to the government in Washington belonged to the individual states and their people.

This idea was called *Nullification* or *Interposition*. It was not original with Calhoun. It had been conceived by Thomas Jefferson and James Madison, as a threat against anti-alien laws, back in the first John Adams administration, and, as a threat, it had worked at that time. Calhoun hoped it might work again, against the protective tariff laws, and thus cause Congress to repeal them. But the North knew perfectly well that if Congress repealed the tariff, the government and the businessmen would lose money. And the political leaders had other worries. Could you run a government in Washington if an individual state could refuse to obey a law? Could an act passed by Congress be lawful in one state and not binding on another?

Andrew Jackson did not think so. He frowned and fretted and chewed down hard on his corncob pipe. He wished he had never heard of John C. Calhoun. Jackson was President of the United States, but he knew he could not run a government unless the principle of Nullification was put down. Someone would have to educate the people. Someone would have to fight Nullification in the Senate of the United States. Andrew Jackson knew this. So did Daniel Webster.

Throughout history, Daniel Webster has been known as "The Defender of the Constitution." He has a right to that name. Like Calhoun, Webster was born a farm boy. But he wasn't built to stay a farm boy. He was a frail youngster, and it was early decided that he must go to school. He got a splendid education at Dartmouth College, in New Hampshire, but this was not what charted the course of his future life.

For when young John C. Calhoun was growing up under his harsh father's teachings, learning suspicion of the Constitution and the federal laws, Daniel Webster was learning reverence for the Constitution. It was a bleak, harsh country where Webster lived as a boy, there in the valley of the Merrimack, scarred with gray ridges and tumbling stone walls. It was a violent country of fierce heat in the summertime, of thunderstorms, and of long, bitter winters when men huddled close around the fireplace and were entertained by a little boy named Daniel, who read Bible verses aloud. These heavy-boned farmers, who plowed with oxen, seemed never to have learned how to smile. Yet, they knew how to love.

They loved this stern country of theirs. Like Webster's own father, a black-haired, black-eyed six-footer who had stormed the breastworks at Bennington, they had wrested this land from the rocks and the Redcoats. They ran their towns themselves, and

Captain Webster was a big man in town affairs: Moderator, Town Clerk, Selectman. It was here in the New England town meeting that Daniel Webster cut his teeth on politics, and learned his love of town and love of state and love of country.

For when he was a little boy, the great struggle was under way for the states to adopt the Federal Constitution. New Hampshire was the last state needed to put the Constitution into action. And around this time, Daniel Webster's father brought home a present for his boy — a pocket handkerchief upon which was printed the Constitution of the new United States. Daniel Webster learned his letters from this handkerchief.

Somehow, though, New Hampshire was too small a place to hold Daniel Webster. He was a New Hampshireman always; he never did forget that rugged country of white-topped hills and clear-running streams. But he went down to the big city of Boston and got elected to Congress. He was in the first rank of the second generation of great American patriots, and his patriotism was nourished in Boston, the "cradle of the American Revolution."

He had a fine house and a big farm at Marshfield, where he could be "Squire" Webster, and watch his guests in their carriages rolling up the long avenue lined with oaks and maples and pine. But he was a countryman still, up before dawn, roaring, and stripping the bedclothes off his children. Then he would be out pitching hay or guiding the huge plow or rowing along a fishing stream, with his red flannel shirt glowing in the sun. He had a fishing rod called Killall, with which he once caught a hundred fish in a day. He had a hundred fat oxen, and they all knew him when he walked by.

As time passed, he became a myth. Stories grew up around him. It was said that he had seen the mighty sea serpent, rearing up out of Buzzards Bay. It was said that he wrestled every morning with his giant ram, Goliath, and that the fish jumped right up out of the streams into his pockets, because they knew it was no use putting up a fight against Daniel Webster. It was said that when his horses died he buried them all saddled and shod and standing up, waiting for Judgment Day. It was even said that he had done battle with the Devil, himself.

"The Godlike Daniel," they called him. No one, it was said, could be quite as great as Daniel Webster looked. He looked like a great man; he talked and acted like a great man — and how he could talk! Men became so excited they thought their heads would burst during his speeches. Yet this was not because of the way Webster spoke, alone. It was because of the way he looked: the stately head crowning the wide sweep of his shoulders, the great, brooding dark eyes, the warm copper glow to his skin.

If John C. Calhoun was in love with the land and the way of life on the land; and Henry Clay loved the American people and the greatness of the people; then Daniel Webster was in love with the Federal Union of the United States. He could not woo and win men to a cause like Henry Clay. He could not work out constitutional theories of government like Calhoun. What he could do was fire men with the idea of the Federal Union, of the greatness of this great country. He could do that because he was on fire with it himself.

Daniel Webster was a giant in his own time, and he became a legend later on. He has been gone a hundred years now and more; yet, according to Stephen Vincent Benét, when the thunder rolls around Marshfield, you can still hear his rolling voice in the hollows of the sky. "Neighbor," he says, "how stands the Union?"

THE
GREAT
DEBATES

4

I<small>T</small> WAS in the winter of
1830 that Daniel Webster became really worried
about Nullification, John C. Calhoun's theory that
a state could refuse to obey a federal law. Half
awake, leaning against a pillar in the Senate Chamber one day, Webster slowly came alive. For days, a
debate had been going on about the ownership of
the public lands, but everyone recognized that more
was involved than the public lands. Daniel Webster
listened . . .

The spokesman for the South was Senator Robert
Young Hayne, of South Carolina. It should have
been Calhoun, but Calhoun was still Vice-President,
and was not allowed to speak. Everybody liked Mr.
Hayne, and this made what he had to say all the more
dangerous. All Washington smiled whenever it saw

Mr. Hayne. He had a velocipede, the ancestor of our present-day bicycle. He scooted all over Washington on that velocipede. The dust blew in clouds, and the children ran in packs, shrieking, and he had himself a very good time.

Now, on the morning of January 21, 1830, Hayne was serious. Slim and erect in a suit of Southern-made homespun, his light-brown hair falling in loose waves over his forehead, his full-lipped mouth smiling, he was still serious. It was almost as if he were an actor in a play.

For days, it had been announced that Daniel Webster and Robert Hayne would debate the cause of the South. For days, people had been arriving in Washington. They filled every little hotel and boardinghouse in town. They argued about Webster and Hayne and Jackson and Calhoun. Now they were all in the Senate gallery, watching and waiting.

Vice-President John C. Calhoun slammed down his gavel, and Hayne got to his feet. The chattering and whispering died away. Daniel Webster waited, his eyes half-closed. But the eyes of the crowd were fixed on John C. Calhoun. He was the real speaker, they knew. And he was excited. He was even paler than usual, and his eyes were very bright. But, as

Hayne's words poured out, he smiled.

Calhoun was busy. You could see his head bent over his desk. He was writing notes to Hayne, telling him what to say. The pageboys kept carrying them down the aisle. Suddenly, Daniel Webster's eyes gleamed. Hayne had said something wrong. It was only a minor point; most people would never have noticed it, but Daniel Webster noticed it. Using Hayne's little mistake, he would be able to tear apart the South Carolina senator's entire argument. He was no longer worried about anything Mr. Hayne had to say.

A few days later, on January 26, it was cold and clear in Washington. Clouds of red dust filled the streets, cutting and stinging the faces of the ladies as they got down from their carriages, and dirtying their little satin shoes. The ladies filled the galleries, and overflowed into seats on the floor, so that several senators had to stand. It was a real fight now, between North and South, Webster and Hayne — or, maybe, Webster and Calhoun.

A famous artist, George Healy, has recaptured this scene in an old painting that hangs in Faneuil Hall, Boston. The glow from the skylight pours down on Webster's massive head. His dark eyes shine out from under the big domelike forehead.

He has his "speaking suit" on, dark blue, with bright brass buttons, and a buff-colored waistcoat. All around him, out of the shadows, the crowded faces are lifted toward the speaker. Looming, too, out of the shadows, is the dark figure of Calhoun, bent over the Vice-President's desk at the left: the clear, hawklike profile, the hair stiff and upstanding, like Andrew Jackson's, the whole lean body tense as a tight spring.

Calhoun was helpless. Webster talked for the better part of two days, and Calhoun could say nothing and do nothing, but the whole meaning of the speech was reflected on his changing face. As Webster attacked Hayne's plea for the agricultural South to unite against the big business interests of the North, Calhoun's face grew more somber. Webster was praising a strong central government that would help industry. He wanted a big government road-building program. Calhoun got more and more excited.

But at Webster's tribute to Massachusetts, to Plymouth Rock, to the beginnings of the America Republic, Calhoun was visibly moved. In the gallery, visitors from Massachusetts began to cry. Webster's dark skin glowed; his eyes burned. Even Calhoun was with Webster now. As Webster felt

about Massachusetts, he felt about South Carolina
. . . the love . . . the pride . . . The Vice-President's
dark eyes were shining with tears.

> When my eyes shall be turned to behold for
> the last time the sun in heaven, may I not see
> him shining on the broken and dishonored
> fragments of a once glorious Union; on States
> dissevered, discordant, belligerent; on a land
> rent with civil feuds, or drenched, it may be,
> in fraternal blood! Let their last feeble and
> lingering glance rather behold the gorgeous
> ensign of the republic, now known and hon-
> ored throughout the earth, still full high
> advanced, its arms and trophies streaming in
> their original lustre, not a stripe erased or
> polluted, nor a single star obscured, bearing
> for its motto, no such miserable interrogatory
> as "What is all this worth?" nor those other
> words of delusion and folly, "Liberty first
> and Union afterwards"; but everywhere,
> spread all over in characters of living light,
> blazing on all its ample folds, as they float over
> the sea and over the land, and in every wind
> under the whole heavens, that other senti-
> ment, dear to every true American heart —
> Liberty *and* Union, now and for ever, one
> and inseparable!

Daniel Webster knew there could be no separation of liberty and union. One was entwined with the other. A sharp rap of the Vice-President's gavel broke the applause. The "Great Debate" was over, and no one who was not there could understand the excitement of that day.

The Great Debate was over, but the fight had just begun.

Like a smoldering bog fire, if quenched here, it would only break out somewhere else. The South would not be downed. Neither would the North. The battle lines would only be redrawn.

As yet, no one knew where President Andrew Jackson stood. He had not said. Jackson was a Democrat, and most of the Southern Democrats were secretly or openly endorsing the Nullification idea. And Andrew Jackson was a Southerner . . .

They determined to smoke him out. The occasion was the annual Jefferson Day dinner in 1830 at the famous Indian Queen Inn. The affair was solidly in the hands of the Southerners. They prepared the toasts, twenty-four of them, all more or less endorsing Nullification. Copies were printed and placed at each plate. A good dinner was served: turkey, duck, partridges and pickled oysters, but nobody was interested in the food.

Jackson arrived with his favorite cabinet officer, Secretary of State Martin Van Buren, at his side. What was the President going to say? No one knew. He sat through the toasts, all twenty-four of them, silent and stern. He and Calhoun sat at opposite ends of the table and looked at each other. Finally came the cry:

"The President of the United States!"

They stood up, the President and the Vice-President, both long, slender, bushy-haired men, towering over most of the others in the room. Martin Van Buren climbed on a chair to see what was going on.

President Jackson raised his glass. "Our Federal Union: it must be preserved." That was all he said. It was all he needed to say.

Calhoun's eyes went black and his hand shook. But when he lifted his own glass, his voice was firm and clear. "The Union," he said, "next to our liberty most dear." He had picked up the challenge. That night, in that room, the battle lines of the Civil War had been drawn.

Events now moved quickly. The South knew there would be no help coming from Andrew Jackson. There would be no help coming from the Senate. So South Carolina proceeded to act on her own. In the fall of 1832 the legislature formally nullified the tariff act, and Andrew Jackson blew up with a roar.

He sat before his untidy desk in the White House study and smoldered with anger. To him, as to Calhoun, the tariff was not the real question. Just what kind of a government was he leading as President? What was to stop every state now from deciding what taxes it wanted to pay, and what laws it chose to obey?

He looked over his reports from South Carolina. Violence was threatening. Charleston was already an armed camp. Young bloods — mounted minute men — marching, drilling, with dueling pistols in their hands.

Jackson called in Secretary of State Edward Livingston, who had succeeded Van Buren. Livingston helped him prepare a proclamation to the "Fellow-citizens of my native state." Sternly, he warned them that "The Constitution forms a government, not a league . . . To say that any state may secede . . . is to say that the United States is not a nation." Disunion, or disobedience to the law, was

Daniel Webster.
A portrait by Alvan Clark

The City of Boston

8   Webster's Reply to Hayne.
Painting by George Healy that Hangs in Faneuil Hall

9   Sam Houston.
    A portrait by Seymour Thomas

treason. Would South Carolina deluge the nation with blood?

Privately, the President's language was even stronger. "Tell them," he sent the word where it would do the most good, "if one South Carolina finger be raised in defiance of this Government, I shall come down there; and . . . hang the first man I lay hands on to the first tree I can reach."

The other Southern states got the idea. Not one dared follow South Carolina's lead. It was not really true that Nullification meant the same thing as secession or war. However, if a state had the constitutional right to nullify a federal law, then it had also the right to secede from the Union. This was not a right that Jackson was prepared to admit.

Andrew Jackson did not understand Calhoun. Calhoun loved the Union no less than he did, but Jackson loved it more simply. He had fought for it since he was a boy of fourteen; he had watered its soil with his blood. Everything else that he had loved was gone. He had never had any children. His beloved wife Rachel was dead; Sam Houston, whom he had looked upon as a son, had gone into exile. The Union was all that Andrew Jackson had left to love, and he would defend it with his last breath and with all the power of his presidential office. He loved the Union for itself; but Calhoun loved it as a symbol of the rights of men and states and the South. A government that ruled by force was no free government. He thought that where a majority ruled unchecked, the minority had lost its freedom; and that justice, the great end and purpose of government, no longer existed.

Jackson's final challenge to South Carolina was the Force Bill, which would compel rebellious states to obey federal law — by force of arms, if necessary. And Calhoun defied Andrew Jackson. Jackson had ordered the Secretary of War to alert the forts in Charleston Harbor. He had named General Winfield Scott in command of army forces to invade South Carolina. He had sent the Force Bill to the Senate, and Calhoun was there to debate it, as Senator from South Carolina, the only man in American history to have resigned the Vice-Presidency. He had met the President's challenge head on.

Tense and overwrought, talking so fast the spectators could hardly follow his words, Calhoun denounced the Force Bill as a declaration of war against South Carolina. It would mean "a massacre of her citizens." In effect, it even repealed the Constitution of the United States. For, if passed, it could be clamped down on any state that dared differ from the government in Washington. It was worse than the tariff; it was far more dangerous.

Spectators looked at each other in wonder. They had never seen Calhoun like this. He was always an emotional speaker, to be sure; some critics even felt that he had more natural "feeling and fire" than Webster. But on this occasion, a reporter observed, his words "seemed to come from his inmost soul and to agitate him from head to foot in their delivery." No one thought him a traitor now. No one could look at him without being moved.

If we were truly a union of states, he demanded, and if the *states* had made the national government, not the people, how could the government force the states to obey? "To preserve this Union by force," Calhoun exploded, ". . . may indeed hold the parts together, but such union would be the bond between master and slave . . ." If the attempt were made, South Carolina would be ready. Thousands of her sons were prepared "to lay down their lives in defence of the State, and the great principles of constitutional liberty for which she is contending."

Calhoun lifted his shaggy head in pride. As a state, he said, South Carolina had helped make this

Union, had helped write the Constitution. Now she claimed only the right to judge for herself what was the law within her own state boundaries.

John Calhoun had raised questions to be long debated in the dark and troubled years ahead. Daniel Webster would offer answers, not so much in terms of constitutional theory as of plain common sense. If Nullification were generally applied, with all the states disobeying the laws, as they saw fit, it would be the end of the Union. We were not in the process of becoming a national, consolidated government, as Mr. Calhoun feared; we had already become one. Logically, perhaps even historically, Calhoun may have been right. But Webster was on the side of the people and the side of the future, and that is a combination hard to beat. Wesbter was speaking for what the great majority of American citizens wanted their government to be.

Whether or not Nullification was constitutional, President Jackson made his position clear on one point. It was illegal. The fine details of the debate were of little interest to him. He said privately, but so the word got around, that if South Carolina committed one illegal act, he would have fifty thousand troops down there within forty days.

Many believed that he would. One senator said

to Henry Clay: "These Carolinians are good fellows, and it would be a pity to let old Jackson hang them."

Henry Clay was not sure. Of one thing, however, he was certain. He did not want a civil war. He wanted to be President; the tariff, hated so much by the Nullifiers of the South, was a big plank in his party's platform; but, like Jackson, he loved the Union above all.

So, in the end, it was Henry Clay, in 1833, as in 1820, who managed the compromise to save the Union, which he and Calhoun and Jackson and Webster all loved in their own ways. He met secretly with Calhoun by night, and worked out details of a compromise tariff program. He announced the result in the Senate. His ambition, he said, was to be the "humble instrument" in the hands of God to reconcile a divided people. When Calhoun arose to pledge his support of the compromise, the galleries resounded with applause.

But the country thundered dissension. The North was angry that, because of threats from the South, the tariff men had backed down. Now, the South had to accept the Force Bill, tariff or no tariff. Discipline must be restored. When the vote was called, every senator from the South but John Tyler walked out in protest. The Force Bill went on the books; as

Calhoun said: "A consolidated nationalistic government has now been legally established under the
bloody act."

Now the superiority of national authority over
states authority had been written into law. Iron-
ically, it was Nullification that had brought this
about. If ever a state rebelled again, the Force Bill
could go into action. South Carolina had won its
fight against the tariff. But the federal government
still maintained its right to pass tariff laws and to
compel their enforcement. The South had lost the
constitutional war.

In March, the state leaders of South Carolina were
meeting in the capital, Columbia, ready to take the
final steps for Nullification and war. They rejected
the "bribe" of a compromise tariff. They contended
that the government had no more right to pass a
mild tariff act than a severe one. They charged that
Calhoun had betrayed his own doctrine and his own
state, and they rammed through a resolution of cen-
sure against him.

Thin, white-faced, exhausted, his clothes splashed
with water and mud, Calhoun stood before them.
He had ridden in the mail coaches seven hundred
miles, night and day, without even stopping for
sleep. His one hope had been to get to Columbia

before action was taken, before bloodshed and civil war.

It had been Calhoun who had instructed the South Carolinians on their "rights." Now he had to tell them that Nullification meant war. Andrew Jackson would not back down. Nullification had been one attempt to create a union of independent sovereign states, and it had failed. But Calhoun would devise other programs. "The struggle," he wrote, "far from being over, has only just commenced."

TALL
TALES
OF
TEXAS

5

THERE WAS a man called
Sam Houston and a country called Texas. In the
1830's and 40's, the eyes of many people in the
United States were fixed upon Texas, the land of the
tall story and the long legend. It sprawled, a kind
of vast subcontinent in America, bigger than the
whole of France or Germany, one quarter as big as
the United States.

For over one hundred years, there was nothing in
the whole United States of America as big as Texas,
as big or as broad or as flat as that sea of green grass,
running out to meet the blue sky, and not a dividing
line to tell where the land ended and the sky began.

On the river boats in the 1830's and 40's, men told
tall tales of Texas: of four hundred acres of cotton

blooming white on a single farm; of oysters as big as your hand, and the air so thick with ducks you could not even see the sky . . .

The story of Texas is pretty much the story of one man — Sam Houston. There were other great Texas heroes, of course: the Indian Scout, Deaf Smith; the giant Jim Bowie, running up a Texas-sized record of knife fights, Indian fights, duels, and so on. There was Davy Crockett, who died at the Alamo; and gentle Stephen Austin, who dreamed of a new world in Texas, where "neither religious, political, nor money-making fanaticism . . . shall ever obtain admission." Stephen Austin had an ideal, but Texas was a reality.

It was Sam Houston who made the dreams and hopes for Texas come true. Sam Houston was a big man for a big country. He stood six feet six in his stocking feet. Andrew Jackson had wanted him to be President, and he did become a president, but not of the United States.

The "reannexation of Texas" was Jackson's life-long dream; that, and a nation stretching from the Atlantic to the Pacific. Sam Houston was the instrument of his purpose.

Andrew Jackson was like a father to Sam Houston, whose own father had died young, when Sam was a boy back in Tennessee. He had been a strange, lonely kind of boy, who loved the woods and the wild, lonely creatures there, and the Indian braves that he fished and hunted with. Even as a teen-ager, he had run off to the woods and the Indians, a book under his arm. He loved the Indians at a time when for most white men "the only good Indian was a dead one."

Houston grew to manhood, a restless, flamboyant personality. He was known as "the best mixer in Tennessee." He loved barn raisings, log rollings, barbecues, and women — and the women loved him. He wore a "gorgeous Indian shirt" below the formal beaver hat of the time. In the War of 1812 he rose to the rank of lieutenant, and was so badly wounded that a doctor refused to take care of him, saying it was useless — he would die.

When he was thirty-five, Sam Houston decided to get married. He picked for his wife a proud Tennessee beauty. He was then Governor of Tennessee. A dark secret arose between them. Within three months they separated, and Houston resigned as Governor. He would never say what had happened. All that he said was: "I do love Eliza."

He withdrew to the woods, to the Cherokees and the Indian father who had "adopted" him, as a boy.

All his life, when his trials were too great to face, Houston retreated to the pagan poetry and the "wild liberty of the Red Man." The Indians named him Co-lon-neh, which means *The Raven.*

At the time Houston left Tennessee, the Cherokees were being pushed back into Arkansas. Now, in defiance of all treaties and pledges, even their lands in Arkansas were being threatened. So Sam Houston labored as an Indian agent, striving to prevent fraud against the Cherokees. He tried to persuade the Indians that the Great White Father in Washington would be just, and tried to persuade the Great Father to keep his country's promise. He was a sort of unofficial ambassador from the tribes to Washington, and from Washington to the tribes.

Wearing a white doeskin shirt and yellow leggings, Sam Houston sat as a member of the National Council of Cherokees. But his eyes were on Texas and the Great Plains. He was dreaming vaguely of a separate Texas Republic, a Western Empire, but this was a dream promptly and flatly squelched by his mentor, Andrew Jackson. Texas must be "reannexed," the President insisted, looking back to an old claim that Texas was part of the original Louisiana Purchase.

However, Texas was indisputably now part of

Mexico, and Mexico had only won its own independence from Spain in 1821. So there was a Spanish flavor to Texas when Sam Houston drifted there in the early 1830's: old adobe towns and white mission churches glittering in the sun, señoritas in black mantillas, the music of soft Spanish voices. Soon all this would be changed. . . . Texas was dotted with "bootleg" squatter towns, often settled by American outlaws. In 1821, the Empire of Mexico had tried to restrict the immigration of Americans to 300 families; it would have been as easy to hold back the tides of the sea. Texas was filling with Americans and American money. In February, 1833, Houston wrote Jackson of the determination of the Texans to form a separate state, and to become annexed by the United States . . . But this was not the time; there were other things going on in 1833.

The Union had almost shattered over Nullification. Now, everyone knew that if the Union did break, slavery was the rock upon which it would crash. Soon the first train would steam into Washington, dropping off the men with the New England accents and the petitions and the tense and determined faces. These were the abolitionists — and their minds were made up, as firmly as the Southerners had already made up their minds. The zeal of many of them was hurting their own cause. In Henry Clay's Kentucky there had been plans for gradual emancipation ever since 1798. Now the attacks of the more radical abolitionists made the Kentuckians so angry that they began to defend slavery, instead. In the White House, Andrew Jackson was trying to hold the Union together. He could not bother about Texas — not now.

Sam Houston could think about nothing else. Texas must be free from Mexico. Wearing a Mexican poncho, he drifted about and surveyed the situation. He recruited troops in neighboring Louisiana. Skirmish after skirmish broke out between the Texans and the Mexicans, who were gradually pushed south of the Rio Grande.

It was 1836 — the year of the "Texas Revolution." The Mexican Empire moved to take action. In February, a call for help came from a beleagured American garrison named the Alamo. "I shall never surrender," the commanding officer, W. Barrett Travis, promised. On March 6, a courier brought a last appeal. The Alamo had been under siege for ten days. "The spirits of my men are high," Travis had written. Sam Houston volunteered to march to the relief of the fortress, although as a military man he had long since warned that the Alamo could not be held. He put on buckskins, high-heeled Texas boots and silver spurs. Then, with four men, he rode off to recruit an Army and to seek out the Mexican commander, Santa Anna.

A few miles along, Houston got off his horse and laid his ear to the ground. (This, he said, was a trick the Indians had taught him.) No vibrations echoed from the depths of the earth. All was dead and still. Houston looked up. It was all over, he said; the Alamo had fallen. As a matter of fact, the last fighting man had died by eight o'clock that morning, even as Houston was reading the appeal from Travis. But he continued his march, picking up recruits along the way. They met the plainsman Deaf Smith, who had with him a young woman, her baby, and a Negro slave belonging to Barrett Travis. These were three of the thirty noncombatants from the Alamo that the Mexicans had spared.

By March 25, there were over 1300 men under Houston's command, restlessly waiting for guns. The rain had been falling steadily. News seeped in of another massacre of American volunteers. The rain-soaked men began to dwindle away. Grimly, Houston continued his march across the huge Texas spaces. At San Jacinto lay a broad stretch of grassy plain, running into a wood of live oaks. Here, Houston set up two guns called the Twin Sisters, and filled them with broken horseshoes. Here, he waited . . .

His men were getting impatient. But Houston had to see his sign, the sign that all Indians see before battle. On the morning of April 21, he saw an eagle flashing its wings against the sun. He mounted a white horse. "Remember the Alamo!" he cried. He had only 700 men left now; Santa Anna had over 1300. Late in the afternoon, Houston and his Texas Volunteers attacked, attacked with long knives and bowie knives, hunting knives and bayonets, and the two cannon filled with broken horseshoes.

The fight lasted only fifteen minutes. It was the worst defeat of an enemy since the American slaughter of the British at New Orleans. In fact, Andrew Jackson himself, the hero of New Orleans, said the victory was even greater, that he had only defended. Houston had attacked.

Houston paid for his victory. His broad chest was peppered with shot. His right leg was shattered. After two weeks, he was moved to New Orleans for treatment, half dead from pain and loss of blood. But he would stay only ten days. Rumors of fresh attacks from the Mexicans brought him back. And that October he became the first President of the Texas Republic.

It was understood, of course, that this job was to be only temporary. Texas was to be formally "recognized" by the United States and then to enter the Union. Somehow, the waiting became longer and longer. It would take a while to work out a treaty of annexation, of course. But President Jackson was even delaying recognition of the new country.

Why? Houston wondered. Why let this windfall, this vast continent of a country, go begging for entry to the American Union? One had to be outside of Texas to really get the answer. It was not Texas that the Yankees of New England saw, nor a brave new republic; but one more extension of the hideous institution of slavery. And Jackson did not want a fight over slavery. He was getting old, and his term of office was nearly at an end. As the biographer of both Jackson and Houston has written, Jackson had wanted Texas all along, "and Houston went there to get it for him." Now Jackson and Houston and Texas and the United States of America would have to wait. And on the last day of his last term, Jackson recognized the Republic of Texas — on March 4, 1837.

The next year, during the administration of President Martin Van Buren, Texas made another try for annexation and was rejected. Meanwhile, the new country was growing and prospering. Sam Houston began to glory in his job. He had a presidential "mansion," a log cabin of two rooms, with a "dog trot" between. Official visitors sat on camp cots and slapped at the flies and mosquitoes. But big Sam Houston had a fine new velvet suit in which to receive visitors, and when he was sworn in for a second term, he even had a first lady, Margaret Lea of New Orleans. She was only twenty, and Houston was nearly fifty, but she had dreamed of him as her romantic hero ever since the battle of San Jacinto. As she said, simply: "He had won my heart."

A blue flag with a single star was whipping in the big winds from the Texas plains, a banner that was to inspire one of the great marching songs of the Confederacy, "The Bonny Blue Flag." Up in Washington John Tyler was President of the United States. Texas was recognized as a country by the great powers, France and England. And Sam Houston was not so sure that he wanted Texas to be annexed to the United States now.

But Houston did not know the determination of President Tyler, nor of his dedicated and fighting

Secretary of State, John C. Calhoun. Calhoun was
no friend of Sam Houston's. They had been enemies for over twenty-five years, ever since the day
when young Sam, wearing nothing but an Indian
blanket and a loincloth, had brought a group of
Indian chiefs in to meet the young Secretary of
War. Houston had never forgotten or forgiven the
dressing down Calhoun had given him. So perhaps
he was not too unhappy when Calhoun had trouble
with the United States Senate and his treaty to
annex Texas.

Then Houston saw a pitiful appeal from a dying
hero, back in Tennessee. In shaky, wavering hand-
writing, old Andrew Jackson put himself squarely at
the side of his long-time enemy John C. Calhoun.
They agreed that defeat of annexation would be
"treason to the South." There were 100,000 Americans there, not including the Negroes. Would
America dare risk seizure of this rich prize by a
European power — perhaps even England?

The Senate was not impressed. To the Northerners, Texas and slavery were one. Sam Houston,
however, threatened that Texas itself could be a
rival power. Was that what the United States
wanted? Texas might expand to the west, even
seize California. It was no use. The Senate would

not be blackjacked into surrender. The treaty was voted down.

The battle was not over. Texas was the red-hot issue of the presidential campaign of 1844. All over the Union, from Maine to the Texas border, men were singing:

> Get out of the way; you're all unlucky.
> Clear the tracks for old Kentucky.

Henry Clay was the one who was unlucky. He loved the Union too much to risk war with Mexico, to risk the bitterness of a divided people: great states like Massachusetts and Ohio were dead-set against annexation. James Knox Polk, the Democratic candidate, took his stand — all out — for Texas, and won the election.

Congress would not budge — not with all the pressure from President Tyler and former President Andrew Jackson and future President James Polk, to say nothing of the Texas President, Sam Houston, whose methods were more devious than the others'.

The Tyler administration was almost over. John C. Calhoun had a month more to serve as Secretary of State, and it was then that he decided on one of the boldest moves of a bold career.

A treaty required a two-thirds majority in the

Senate. Calhoun knew he could not get it. So he decided to ask simply for a resolution from Congress, a joint resolution, annexing Texas, which required only a simple majority vote from the House and the Senate. He could get votes enough for that.

Candles were burning on the night of March 3, 1845. Only a few hours before their terms were over, President John Tyler and Secretary of State John C. Calhoun signed the bill that formally invited Texas into the American Union. It would be a year before all the formalities were completed, and Sam Houston would stand, head bared, to receive the lowered blue flag. But the job had been done. "I congratulate Texas and the United States," wrote Andrew Jackson.

Once more, there was talk of Sam Houston for the Presidency. He was, of course, the first senator to be elected from the new state of Texas, but even the debates of the oncoming fight for union wearied him after his great days as chief of the Republic of the Lone Star. Silently, he would sit in the Senate, and ceaselessly his knife would move, as he carved out wooden toys for his children.

Also, in June, 1845, he had a pledge to redeem. He had a journey to make. So did Andrew Jackson.

Houston took his oldest boy with him. They rode

night and day, up from the wide plains into the green forests of Tennessee, in the young country and the late spring. They arrived too late at the Hermitage. Waves of sobbing broke across the stillness of the night.

Sam Houston walked into a room where candles burned around a long figure that had never rested except in death. For minutes he stood, with his head bowed. Then he drew his boy toward the coffin.

"My son," he said, "try to remember that you have looked upon the face of Andrew Jackson."

THE
FIGHT
FOR
UNION

6

IT WAS snowing in Washington.

It was snowing as it had on that night in 1820, but the thin, tall man, pushing his way through the drifts, was old now. The weight of his years lay heavy upon him, and his forebodings lay heavy upon his heart. The man was Henry Clay.

Thirty years before, he had gone out into the night and the snow to seek a compromise that would save the Union. Now he was on his way again to seek help to save the Union, but was he already too late? This was not the young country he had grown up in, with hopes as broad as the great prairies to the westward. This was a dark and troubled Washington he had come back to in the fall of 1849, and like Calhoun, he could ask: "What can one man do?"

Yet he was still Henry Clay, "Harry of the West," graceful and tall, with the same light, springy step, the same smile at the corners of his lips, the same outstretched hand, and in his voice the courtesy and the music of an earlier age. "I am grateful to you, sir," he would say to a visitor, "for coming to see me."

Henry Clay, in a formal, black frock coat and satin waistcoat, his high collar scraping the tips of his ears, had held court that fall at the National Hotel. He had returned to the Senate, as he put it, "to pour oil on the troubled waters." He had come out of retirement at his beloved Ashland in Kentucky, had started his journey to Washington, had heard the wheels spin, had looked back at the blue grass and the golden leaves falling, and then forward into the unknown — the uncertain future of his country.

This Washington, this Senate — this was not the Congress and the capital city that he had known. Pistols and knives were flashing in the House of Representatives. There were threats and fist fights; it took seventeen ballots to elect a Speaker. Now, the more radical abolitionists even claimed the right of Congress to abolish slavery in the old slave states, the states that had written the Constitution and formed the Union. Henry Clay was born when, in the strife of revolution, the Union was born. Would he live now to see its death?

Even the Senate Chamber no longer looked the same. The old stoves were there, steaming with their loads of hickory wood. But gaslights had been installed since Clay's time. They cast a lurid glow across the red draperies and carpets. They turned Daniel Webster into a statue of bronze, and John Calhoun into one of marble, as he sat motionless, scarcely breathing, with only his dark, deep-socketed eyes alive.

The lights glowed upon the ruddy face of Sam Houston, former President of the Republic of Texas, now wrapped in an Indian blanket and whittling time away as the Union fell into splinters around him. Old Tom Benton was there, too; and younger faces, faces new to Henry Clay: William Seward, Stephen A. Douglas, Jefferson Davis, and the young "fire-eaters" of the Deep South, who openly and boldly dared declare now: "The Union is at an end." Mr. Clay would not believe this. To him, the Union was dearer than South or state,

10 Andrew Jackson in his old age.
    A photograph

11 Henry Clay in his later years.
    A photograph

12   John C. Calhoun in his later years.
A portrait by Hix in the South Carolina State Library

or even the cause of freedom itself. To save the Union was his single aim.

He filled his days and evenings at the National Hotel with interviews. He tried to get the agreement of the best minds available. Concessions had to be made by both the North and the South. Slowly, Clay worked them out . . .

California was hammering for admission at the door of the Union. To admit California as a free state would appease the North, for it would give the free states a controlling majority in the United States Senate. With this power, the North would win the struggle of a generation, to abolish the slave trade in Washington, D.C. But the South was to be assured in its turn that slavery itself would never be abolished in Washington without the consent of Maryland and Virginia. As for the new territories of Utah and New Mexico, their land was not adapted to the slavery system, so if the question there was left to the settlers, both North and South would be satisfied. For the South, Mr. Clay called for a stiffening of the Fugitive Slave Law, with ironclad guarantees, assuring the return of all runaway slaves.

Stephen A. Douglas and Sam Houston called at the National Hotel to pledge their support to the plan. But there was one, whose aid was essential, whose help Mr. Clay would have to seek personally. That was why he was out on a wild and storm-swept winter night, making his way toward the Washington home of Daniel Webster.

They sat up a long time that night, two men who had been young together, and now were old together. Henry Clay leaned forward eagerly, his nervous hands moving, his sensitive face a mirror of his eagerness. Daniel Webster sat silent, his great head sunken, his deep eyes brooding. For Henry Clay's words were facing him with the biggest decision of his life.

Daniel Webster still wanted to be President of the United States. He knew that if he supported Mr. Clay, not one Massachusetts congressman would stand with him. He knew that his whole state might turn against him, for the people of Massachusetts would make no compromise with slaveholders; they loved freedom even more than they loved the Union. Yet, to Daniel Webster's credit, let it be said that he hesitated for only one minute. He drank from the jug that stood between them. Then he nodded his head. The plan, he said, would appeal to all reasonable men.

John C. Calhoun, sick in his bed at Hill's boarding house, heard the news of Webster and Clay's

meeting and mused, bitterly. He was convinced that
the time for compromise was over. He, too, loved
the Union, and without his influence the South
might have seceded in 1847, over the Wilmot Proviso, which would have kept all slavery out of the
territories. He had helped beat the Proviso down.
But, afterwards, when he and Stephen A. Douglas
and Jefferson Davis had tried to get Congress to
extend the line of the Missouri Compromise to
the Pacific, they were defeated.

Henry Clay had determined to fight public opinion. He wanted to fight hatred of slavery with love
of country. He wanted people to think about what
they loved, not about what they hated. He keyed
himself up to so high a pitch that his physical
strength buckled. On the wintry morning of his
scheduled speech, he stood at the foot of the Capitol
steps, then said to a friend: "Will you lend me your
arm? I feel quite weak and exhausted today."

His friends begged him not to make the speech;
fiercely, he shook them off. "Our country is in danger," he said, "and if I can be the means of saving
her, my health or my life is of little consequence."
A wave of applause broke over him, as he stood up;
no one who saw him was unmoved. He held his
frail figure erect, but he looked all of his seventy-

three years. The beautiful musical voice kept breaking; yet he spoke for almost two days. All who watched him and heard him knew that they were looking at history.

"Let us go to the altar of our country," Henry Clay pleaded, "and swear that ... we ... will uphold her Constitution; that we will preserve her Union ... I know no North, no South, no East, no West." He said: "This Union is my country; the thirty states are my country; Kentucky is my country ... if my own state should raise the standard of disunion, I would go against her ... much as I love her."

Next came Sam Houston of Texas, the first national leader to speak out for the Clay compromise. His thinking was as broad as his body was long. When he had been a boy in the 1790's, he pointed out, it was just naturally assumed that one day slavery would come to an end. Then the demand for cotton and cotton prosperity had reversed the pattern. Northern intermeddling had done the rest, solidifying Southern resistance.

Sam Houston was for compromise. Like Clay, he could say: "I know neither North nor South; I know only the Union." He shouted: "Think you ... after the difficulties Texans have encountered to get into the Union, that you can whip them out of it?"

The news that John C. Calhoun was preparing a speech cast a pall of gloom over the spirits of those who hoped for compromise. His address was set for March 4, 1850, and a kind of shiver went over the hall of Congress as he entered and stood for a moment, glancing proudly about the Senate Chamber, where he had ruled for so long. A few in the gallery could still remember him and his colleagues, forty years before, vital and young, as young as their young country.

Tears stung their eyes, for now Calhoun was too weak even to stand alone. He sat by, like a ghost, as his speech was read aloud for him, his shaggy head drooping, his hands clutching the arms of his chair. Death was written on Calhoun's face, and there were some who heard in his words the death knell of the South and of the old Federal Union.

John C. Calhoun would have no part of compromise. Compromise could not halt the great civil war that he saw coming. The wounds had gone too deep. From the first, he had believed that the agitation of the slavery question would split the Union. Year by year, he had watched the slow undermining of the Constitution. Year by year, he had watched the Federal Union, based on states' rights, changing into "a great national consolidated democracy," with power centered in the hands of the President.

Once, there had been a kind of balance between the two sections. Now, Calhoun felt, the South had lost the power to protect itself against the power of the North in Congress. And, as final judge of its own power, the North, in time, could end slavery by force; or ruin the South by economic pressures.

What, then, did Calhoun think could be done? "The Constitution is my letter of instruction," he had said, back in the era of 1812. The Constitution was all that he had to offer now. Only a constitutional amendment, not a compromise, could save the South and the Union together. And such an amendment could be passed only if the North feared disunion more than it hated slavery. Yes, the Union could be saved, Calhoun insisted, but only if the North put its love of a united country ahead of its concept of moral law.

He had had his say. This was Calhoun's last great effort, although he appeared, ghostlike, a few more times in the Senate, sitting by, brooding, during Webster's great speech a few days later. Within three weeks he was dead, burned out by his anxiety and hopelessness and unresting, tormented vision. "The South, the poor South," was always in his mind. To many, his death seemed symbolic of the cause of the South that he had served so long. Yet almost his last words were of the Union. "If I had my health and my strength," he said, "to give one hour in the Senate, I could do more for my country than at any time in my life.

Daniel Webster, speaking on the 7th of March, had girded himself for the supreme trial of his life. He was against the spread of slavery. His own Massachusetts had nullified the fugitive slave laws within the state. But the Senator from Massachusetts was still Daniel Webster, the Defender of the Union. "I wish to speak today, not as a Massachusetts man, nor as a Northern man, but as an American," he said. "I speak today for the preservation of the Union. 'Hear me for my cause.' "

Outside, it was very cold. Inside, it was stifling. The Senate Chamber was jammed, the galleries, the hallways, the cloakrooms; the crowding was so great that even the senators could hardly get to their seats. Many people had been traveling for many days and hundreds of miles. They wanted to look a last time on that majestic figure in the blue-tailed coat, with the great domed forehead and brooding eyes. They wanted to hear that organlike voice once more.

Would there be peace or war? "The imprisoned winds are loose," Webster said. He called on the nation to breathe the "fresh air of liberty and union." He pleaded: "Let us not be pygmies when the time calls for men." There was applause when he finished. It was almost the last applause of his life.

Yes, Daniel Webster had saved the Union. Even the South admitted that. All over the South newspapers echoed the words of the Charleston *Mercury*. Mr. Calhoun's speech would have been decisive, the *Mercury* said, had it not been followed so soon by Mr. Webster's noble and generous words. To the South, Daniel Webster *was* the North, the North offering compromise. When Daniel Webster had stopped speaking, the United States was one country again.

But he had divided his Northern supporters, as well as the Southern extremists. Exactly as he had foreseen, he had destroyed himself politically. Boston's foremost clergyman, the Reverend Theodore Parker, even charged Webster with having corrupted the conscience of the nation. New England's best-known poet, John Greenleaf Whittier, labeled him the lost and fallen Ichabod. He was damned in Boston's historic old Faneuil Hall as a Lucifer, a Benedict Arnold, and "a traitor to the cause of freedom."

Webster did not falter. He echoed the words of Henry Clay. No man could suffer too much, if it was in defense "of the liberties and Constitution of his country." In troubled times, it was far easier to fan the flames of controversy. He planned to take the stump in every village in New England, if need be, to change the minds of his people, but he lacked the strength. His course was run.

Within two years, he lay dying in his bedroom at Marshfield. Day and night, his eyes rested on the American flag, flying from the masthead of a little boat he had anchored on the pond, and lighted in the dark by a ship's lantern. He had written his own epitaph: "I shall stand by the Union." And when the news of his death came, all the flags in the country dipped to half-mast. Ralph Waldo Emerson, who had condemned him, saw him as "a masterpiece like Napoleon." In New Hampshire and in Massachusetts and in all the thirty states, men wondered how the sun would rise or life go on in a country without Daniel Webster.

Life went on. The country went on. The effect

of Webster's mighty effort had swung the tide. There was still opposition to compromise, of course, even from patriotic men. Big, blustering Thomas Hart Benton, of Missouri, "a wild buffalo of a man," a determined and defiant patriot, claimed that the Compromise of 1850 was unfair to the North. There was no need for compromise. There were more important questions than slavery. "California is suffering for want of admission . . . New Mexico is suffering for want of attention . . . Congress is suffering for want of progress in business."

Benton, like others, paid the penalty of his patriotism. After thirty years in the Senate, Missouri retired him. His warlike calls for peace shocked even his warmest admirers. Ten years later, his voice from the grave, like Clay's, would hold a divided and prostrate, but loyal, Missouri in the Union.

The great Compromise debates continued through two years. Henry Clay, weary, irritable, but undaunted, fought on. Over and over, he repeated: "I am against agitators, North and South." He spoke at least seventy times. Sometimes he was too weak even to stand, for tuberculosis, the disease that had killed Calhoun, had fastened its deadly grip upon him.

Yet through the spring and ghastly heat of a

Washington summer, he fought on — with all the eloquence, the charm, the power of that personality which defeat had mellowed, but never embittered. He lived to see the battle won. The actual Omnibus Bill, as it was called, was voted down on paper. But its separate provisions were rewritten, passed, and became the law of the land.

In the spring of 1852, Henry Clay lay dying in his room in the National Hotel. In far-off Boston, the city that had damned Daniel Webster, a 100-gun salute now boomed out in tribute to the Compromise, and a headline read: "The country saved."

Henry Clay's work was done. It had been nearly fifty years since he first came to Washington. He could remember the Founding Fathers . . . their faces . . . Jefferson . . . Madison . . . Adams . . . John Quincy Adams, his near and dear friend. If he could only see the colts running in the blue grass, smell the scent of Kentucky roses, or talk to his wife once more. It was not to be; he never left his room again. And years later, a man called Abraham Lincoln would declare that this country could never have been what it had become without Henry Clay.

Was it a useless battle after all? Webster and Clay and Sam Houston had saved the Union, in a sense, against its own will. This was the tragedy. Webster and Clay and Calhoun, Houston and Benton and Andrew Jackson were among the greatest men this country had produced since the Founding Fathers. Yet, even they were not enough. As leaders, they defied the will of the people, to do what they thought best for the people's safety and welfare. What the people want is what counts, and neither then nor now can any law be upheld over the will of the people to defeat it.

The tragedy was that each side, North and South, was convinced that it was right. The South was legally right on the question of states' rights, and the North was morally right on the question of slavery. To both sides, a single inch of compromise was mortally wrong. As slavery had become more essential to Southern prosperity, it had become more and more distasteful to Northern morality. Southerners saw the Constitution as guaranteeing their rights in slavery; Northerners saw the Constitution as guaranteeing the rights of free men. No political issue could be viewed in its own terms. When Southerners wanted to migrate west, Northerners saw this as nothing but a plot to extend slavery. When Northerners wanted western lands opened for a transcontinental railroad, Southerners saw this as a plot to extend Northern control. No common point of view was possible because there was no more common ground.

Calhoun had been right in his conviction that no compromise would work, because you cannot compromise a question of moral principle. Slavery and states' rights had become moral principles. Not even the Union mattered so much in the end as what each side thought the Union meant to be.

What Webster and Clay and Houston had done was to make sure that the Northern ideal would prevail. They had not saved the Union forever. They had not halted that "irrepressible conflict" that they foresaw and tried so hard to avoid. Their Compromise did not last; it scarcely endured four years. But it gave the North time, as the whole country slid slowly and inevitably down the precipice . . .

One member of the Great Generation was left to watch the explosion of the nation he had grown up with and had so dearly loved — Sam Houston. He had been the President of a free republic that he had brought into a greater republic, and now he saw all his hopes and dreams shattered. He was a lame-duck senator, repudiated and voted out by the Texans back home, his punishment for his support of the Compromise. But he still fought on.

Massive and towering, he stood beneath the gaslights and the eagle of the American Republic, draped in black for the passing of Webster and Clay. Would it soon be draped for the passing of the Republic itself? He could remember Washington in ruins after the War of 1812. Would he live to see it so again?

He never saw Washington again. Defeated, he went home and ran for Governor of Texas. "The last of his race . . . the Texas Trojan," they called him. Up and down that mighty continent of a state, he tramped. "I a traitor to Texas?" he roared. He ripped open his shirt, bared his chest, scarred with the wounds of San Jacinto. "I have watered it with my blood."

He won, and his victory stirred reverberations across the Union. He was the first Union man in the South to win an election since Clay's time; it was the first setback for the Southern extremists in ten years. What the North did not know was that it was not a Union victory. It was a personal victory.

Sam Houston was becoming an old man; he was almost seventy. Soon he could no longer rule by sheer hypnotic power. Facing a Texas mob that threatened his life, he stood, his deep-set eyes staring the would-be Confederates down. He predicted: "You may, after the sacrifice of countless millions and hundreds of thousands of lives . . . win Southern independence . . . but I doubt it . . . the North is determined to preserve this union."

In the end, Texas entered the Southern Confederacy, but without Sam Houston. He had refused to take the oath of allegiance to the new government, and the office of Governor was declared vacant.

In a final proclamation, Houston explained: "I love Texas too well to bring strife and bloodshed upon her . . . I will not yield those principles I fought for . . ." He died with the gunfire of the Civil War echoing about him, murmuring the word "Texas" over and over again like a litany.

WIND
FROM
THE
NORTH

7

In THE crisis-year of 1858 a man of twenty-nine was wandering through the prairie country of the Middle West, looking and listening. His name was Carl Schurz. He was a foreigner — a refugee, later generations might have called him — and as a future army general, cabinet officer, and senator of the United States, he was to become perhaps the most distinguished newcomer America was to welcome. He was part of an onsurging tide. Back in his native Germany, he had been one of the fiery, fighting spirits that had set the country ablaze in the Revolution of 1848. But the revolt had failed. Schurz had fled with a price on his head.

Now, Carl Schurz and thousands of other freedom-

Daniel Webster.
A photograph made in 1851

loving young Germans were flooding into the main
stream of American life, pouring across the prairie
states, bringing new names into the American herit-
age. Yet, this was not the only mass migration. In
ten years' time the American population would leap
from 23 million to 31 million. Hungry, freedom-
loving Irish were swarming off the boats at Boston;
soon the people of Italy and Middle Europe would
be on their way. Perhaps young Carl Schurz heard
the story of Henry Clay, on a trip home from Washington. He had leaped from the stage, knelt down,
and put his ear to the ground.

"What are you listening for, Mr. Clay?" someone
asked.

"I was listening to the tread of unnumbered
thousands of feet that are to come this way westward," he had answered.

Westward, the people were moving, Conestoga
wagons swaying and creaking, their white tops shining like girls' bonnets in the sun, rail lines running
westward, always westward. The larger part of
America now lay to the west; it was an area bigger
than all the free states. This was indeed a great and
growing country that young Carl Schurz looked
upon. A continent was moving westward, but what
was it moving toward — freedom or slavery? Which

would this vast land be? Here, as in Germany, freedom was on trial; and dark questions waited, to which no man had the answer.

There were other problems for Americans to debate and consider in those growing years of the 1850's: the railroad bills, the homestead bills, free farms and free land, unemployment, laboring conditions, the tariff — but one question was uppermost in the minds of the American people and of young Carl Schurz: that of freedom or slavery. And as he listened, he heard many voices . . .

The law was plain. The law read: "That when a person held to service or labor in any State or Territory . . . shall escape . . . the person or persons to whom such . . . labor may be due . . . may pursue or reclaim such fugitive person." This was the Fugitive Slave Act, a part of the great Compromise of 1850. When it was passed, cannon had thundered across the South, but one Northern senator had said: "The echoes they awaken shall never rest until slavery itself shall die." Congressman Joshua Giddings called the act "unconstitutional . . . abhorrent . . . barbarous . . ." Massachusetts passed "Personal Liberty Laws," outlawing and nullifying the new Fugitive Slave Act in the Commonwealth.

On March 6, 1857, the Supreme Court brought

things to a head. In the famed Dred Scott case, it ruled that no slave could be a citizen with the right to sue in the courts; and that Congress had no right to exclude slavery from a territory, and therefore, the Missouri Compromise was unconstitutional. The Court, at least, vindicated John C. Calhoun. But the North refused to accept the Supreme Court's decision. The decision must be reversed, declared the New York *Tribune*. The new Republican party went on record that slavery itself was "a great moral, social, and political evil," and demanded repeal of the Fugitive Slave Law. Meanwhile, the voices were sounding . . . louder . . . ever louder . . .

Along the foothills of the Appalachian Mountains, along the line where Mason and Dixon had marked the boundary between slavery and freedom, dark shadows of men moved, traveling by night and the North Star. Far-off, winter-locked Canada was their destination; since the Dred Scott decision there was no place of freedom or safety for them in the free United States. A new term, "the Underground Railway," was whispered into the American language. Fugitive slaves were hidden behind potato sacks in cellars, under the hay in barns; in Galesburg, Illinois, they were even hidden in a church steeple. The

Underground Railway — this was an answer and a protest from free Americans against the Supreme Court and the Fugitive Slave Law. Still another wedge had been driven to split the American people apart.

And still another voice was sounding. M·s. Harriet Beecher Stowe of Brunswick, Maine, was a little woman of forty, the mother of six children. Once she had lived near the Ohio River, and had visited a slave plantation in Kentucky. She had been in Boston at the height of the abolitionist crusade, and had heard the story of a fleeing Negro mother who had jumped overboard from a river steamboat with her baby in her arms. Mrs. Stowe had decided to "write something." The first chapter of *Uncle Tom's Cabin* came to her in church one morning, and her family wept at the reading of it.

Uncle Tom's Cabin was the biggest best-seller since the Bible. Eight presses were put to work printing it; and the North became all the more convinced that there were two ways of life and two kinds of people in the United States: good Northerners and bad Southerners. North and South, public opinion was stiffening. North and South, the battle between freedom and slavery was being fought out: in words on the prairies of Illinois, in vicious pitched battles on the plains of Kansas and Nebraska. "Bleeding Kansas" had already become a symbol of the Union "bleeding at every pore," as Calhoun had foreseen. And yet, there were still voices sounding . . .

Stephen A. Douglas of Illinois had offered an an-swer. The biggest man in Congress in the 1850's was a little man, Senator Stephen A. Douglas, who stood only five feet three inches high. He was blue-eyed and intense, with a great rolling voice and a shaggy lionlike head topping his small body. He was a Democrat and a "whole-hog Jackson man." He dreamed of a country stretching from ocean to ocean. Agitation of the slavery question, he thought, was interfering with the growth of America. "This tornado," he said, "has been raised by abolitionists and abolitionists alone."

Douglas also blamed the politicians. His idea was to get the politicians out of the slavery ques-tion, to leave the solution up to the people, and to the natural forces of geography and history. "Let there be popular sovereignty," Douglas had cried.

He had written his idea into the Kansas-Nebraska bill for the "settlement" of the two new territories. Kansas and Nebraska could be either slave or free, depending on who got there first and how the set tlers voted. This pleased the South, for, in theory, it opened all northern territory, not yet admitted as states, to slave property. It outraged the North for the same reason. Being both a politician *and* a man who loved his country, Douglas tried to heal the rift.

He tried to argue that the Kansas-Nebraska Act would work for both sides. According to the Dred Scott decision, Southerners had a legal right to take their slaves into Kansas and Nebraska, or into any other territory. But if the Northern settlers refused to pass laws to protect those slaves, who would risk taking them there? A program intended to please everybody of course pleased nobody, and four years after the Kansas-Nebraska Act had become law, debate still raged over it. By the summer of 1858, Douglas had his back to the wall. He was fighting, not only for re-election to the United States Senate, but for his political survival, and for the survival of a country and a party in which two opposing ideas could exist side by side. Stephen A. Douglas was the nation's foremost Democrat. You could not be a Democrat in the 1850's and please Northerners and Southerners alike. Stephen A. Douglas was trying to do this. Countering him was his opponent for the United States Senate, Republican Abraham

Lincoln. No one had ever seen anything quite like the Illinois debates between the little-known, one-term Congressman Lincoln and Senator Stephen A. Douglas of Illinois.

This was America, these great plains and crowded little towns, these Great Debates, these combinations of barbecue and picnic and hog-calling contest . . . this was America, these rows of buckboards and buggies . . . the youngsters eating watermelon, the smells of hot gingerbread and the cries of the hawkers . . . the farm wives on the wagons, upright and silent beneath their great sunbonnets, the two stout fellows wrestling . . . the band tootling "Listen to the Mockingbird," "My Darling Clementine" and "Yankee Doodle," and Abraham Lincoln stripping off his coat to "let 'er rip," in the hot blaze of an August sun.

They were an oddly assorted pair, Lincoln and Douglas, any way you looked at it. Douglas, the "Little Giant" with the big voice, was much better known. He made up in sound what he lacked in stature, roaring, gesturing, beating his chest, clenching his fists as he talked and once even ripping off his shirt.

And Lincoln was a tall rack of bones with a black suit dangling on it, with a long, black hat like a stovepipe, almost a foot high. He looked like a farmer and he drawled like a farmer, and his trousers were worn and shiny where he had twisted his hands around his knees and tugged at them. His long legs looked as though you could fold them up somewhere; he looked as though he had had longer distances to travel than most men, and had come a longer way. He carried a bulging green umbrella and a woolen shawl for an overcoat over one arm. He looked like an out-of-scale drawing of himself. But it was not how he looked, but how the people felt about him that mattered.

You felt things somehow, listening to that "homely phrase," to that penetrating voice. You might have known him only a few minutes, but you had the feeling that you had known him all your life. And when he talked, men listened.

They listened because they could feel more in him than just the words he was saying. He talked like a neighbor among neighbors, voicing the thoughts that might be swapped at the country store, the thoughts that men felt, but did not dare speak. Behind those thoughts was the reading that he had done: the Bible, Shakespeare, the writings of the Founding Fathers. Out of these profundities he had distilled simplicity. He could put great truths into

The Bettmann Archive

15 Stephen A. Douglas.
A photograph by Matthew Brady

16 Abraham Lincoln.
A photograph probably made in 1860

New Hampshire Historical Society

ILLINOIS BORN UNDER THE ORDINANCE OF '87.

The Bettmann Archive

17 A drawing made at the time of the Lincoln Douglas
Debates.

18 John Brown.
A portrait by N. B. Onthank

words whose impact all could feel, and whose meaning everyone could understand.

The real problem, he repeated, over and over again, went far beyond the Kansas-Nebraska bill. It was not so much a question of how to handle slavery as of slavery itself. The point was that the Northern people looked upon slavery as wrong and the Southern people looked upon it as right. If slavery were right, Lincoln insisted, the North could not object to its being spread across the country, from state to new state. But if it were wrong, the South could not insist upon extending it a single inch.

Abraham Lincoln was convinced that slavery was wrong. Audiences listened to him in great halls where his eyes lighted and his voice went gentle in a quiet so great you could hear the gas jets sizzling. They listened in the prairie towns of Illinois, as Lincoln stood among them, a tall, lanky man in the hazy autumn of 1858, his body swaying as hundreds of white handkerchiefs fluttered at him.

He estimated the value of the slaves as between a thousand million and two billion dollars. To a great extent, popular opinion was based on the value of property. This was understandable. He had no prejudice against the Southern people. "They are just what we would be in their situation." He hated slavery, but he did not hate Southerners; there was no hatred in him. You always had the feeling, as you listened, that here was a man who would like to treat his foe as his friend.

What it all boiled down to, Lincoln told the Illinois audiences, was a question of common humanity, and the rights of common humanity. He had read in a lawbook once that a Negro slave was not legally a person but a *thing*. So he could not agree with Senator Douglas that "if you do not object to my taking my hog to Nebraska, I must not object to your taking your slave. Now I admit this is perfectly logical, if there is no difference between hogs and slaves." But, if you could legally make a *thing* out of a Negro, Lincoln would argue, how long would it be before they began to make *things* out of poor white men? Once, America had believed all men equal. Now, the right to enslave others was being called "a sacred right of self-government."

Lincoln was answering questions not for the answering, but to make his points. The Kansas-Nebraska bill had not really solved anything. It had only turned the territories into a cockpit. So what he wanted to know was this: was there any legal way that the people of a territory, before it became a state, could exclude slavery?

This was a question that Mr. Douglas could answer only in two ways, and both would be wrong. If he said "No," he would be proved a liar on everything he had told the North that "popular sovereignty" could do. If he said "Yes," he would be defying the Dred Scott decision and the Supreme Court, and would lose his Southern support for the presidential nomination in 1860. Mr. Lincoln waited . . . Mr. Douglas said "Yes."

Later, at Galesburg, twenty thousand people from Spoon River and Cedar Fork Creek and the little prairie towns beyond sat in a chill, wet wind from the north, as Lincoln and Douglas talked to them for three hours. Their faces were reddened from the wind. They were grave with thought. Their muscles were bunched from hauling water and guiding plows and finding their own kind of freedom on the heavy Illinois earth.

Before speaking, Lincoln had drunk a cup of coffee and eaten mince pie, and stretched his long legs as if to loosen them. He laughed into the face of a man six feet four inches tall. "Well, you're up some."

Now, he was not laughing. His voice was musing, dreaming almost. He was talking of the past . . . We would have to go back, back to the basic principles of the Founding Fathers, "that slavery was to be restricted and ultimately ended."

He was talking moderation where no moderation was possible. To agitators, North *and* South, he would say: "We won't go out of the Union and you shan't." From first principles, he was denying two basic premises of the South: that because slavery had been recognized from the beginning, it could be continued to the end; and that because the Union had been made by states, it could be unmade by them.

Lincoln had said repeatedly that the Missouri Compromise should be restored. "For the sake of the Union, it ought to be restored." (On that ground, he and John C. Calhoun could have met.) But he knew it would not be restored. He knew, as Jefferson had known, that a line of geography could not coincide with a moral principle. Even before the debates, he had faced the truth, and spoken the words the country had trembled to hear. "A house divided against itself cannot stand." This nation could not endure "half slave and half free." It would become all one.

To a friend now, he added, "I see the storm coming and I know His hand in it."

THE
POWDER
KEG
EXPLODES

8

WHILE LINCOLN and Douglas were debating in Illinois, trying through words to bring some order into the chaos around them, the wounded and scarred new state of Kansas was emerging from the smoke of battle. There, shooting had already taken the place of words. There, in the wake of the tragic Kansas-Nebraska Act, the people themselves had had the responsibility of deciding whether freedom or slavery would prevail in the territory soon to become a state. The people had fought it out with bullets and blood in the 1850's. Their battleground was Kansas.

Kansas, with the rolling gray grass of early winter fading into horizons of lavender and silver-gray, an infinity of flatness, broken by the occasional blur of a cottonwood tree, or a cabin — smoke had blurred those flat horizons. Smoke had swirled across the prairie, flames mounting — red as blood, the flames of barns burning and cornfields — in every direction south of the Kansas River. And out of the smoke and the flame, moving like a reaper across the burning fields, was the figure of a man named John Brown.

John Brown was a quivering, burning torch of a man, with a gray beard like smoke and eyes like coals. "Old John Brown," they always called him; it was as if he had been born old, this man in his vigorous late fifties. You could never imagine him young somehow, a boy. And yet he had been a boy, bareheaded and barefooted in buckskins, back on the Ohio frontier, tending his father's cattle.

He had been a boy who had loved birds and squirrels and had wept when his pet lamb had died. He had been a boy who saw a friend cruelly beaten with an iron shovel because he was a Negro and a slave. A fire had burned through the soul of John Brown. Slavery, he had resolved, must be wiped from the land. "I hold God in infinitely greater reverence than Congress," he once said. He said: "One man and God can overturn the Universe."

He had ridden into Kansas on a wagonload of guns; boxes of rifles marked "Books" followed him.

You would see him in the hotel dining room in Lawrence, a stately man, gaunt and tall, with a floating beard and the look of one accustomed to the woods. "Unfaltering resolution" was stamped on his features. He had his followers, a few young men who did his will almost as if they had lost any will of their own. One of them said: "He possessed that strange power which enables one man to impress many with his views . . . Had John Brown sent a man on an errand to Hades, he must have started thither, for Brown was one of God's own commanders."

The slaveholders swarmed into Lawrence; they burned and sacked the town. John Brown decided what he had to do. He prayed with his family, night and morning; he prayed before every meal. Then he gathered together four of his sons and two followers and told them that he was "a chosen instrument in the hands of God to war against slavery."

The group moved on to Pottawatomie Creek, burning barns and killing five Southern sympathizers. Not a barn, not a herd, not a man was spared. One of his young followers protested the slaughter; Brown shook his head. It was better that innumerable slaveholders should die, he said, rather than one free man. Grimly, he moved on . . . He saw two young men lying dead, with twenty bullet and buckshot wounds in them. One of these was his own son.

Missouri offered $3000 (a lot of money in those days) for his capture. In the winter of 1858 he moved straight into Missouri, charming eleven slaves away like a Pied Piper. His sheer, monomaniac courage was like an invisible shield around him; none dared stand in his way. It was obvious that he thought it "nothing to die in a good cause."

When the battle in Kansas was over, it was equally obvious that John Brown had won it. What he always wanted, he said, was to make slavery so unsafe that it would be unprofitable. Federal troops had had to come into Kansas, and for all practical purposes slavery was almost abolished there. In Missouri, the value of slave property had dropped by a million dollars.

His work in Kansas done, John Brown dropped from sight, but no one missed him. The nation was stiffening for the struggle, for what William H. Seward called "the irrepressible conflict."

History stopped once at Harpers Ferry in western Virginia. Time stopped there, too; it never moved on again. Harpers Ferry is a shell today, gutted and empty, with scarcely eight hundred people scattered through the dusty-brick houses up the hill. Below, the two narrow streets, stretched along a shelf at the base of the bluff, are like a deserted set upon a stage. It is a haunting and a haunted spot.

It is a hundred years and more now since the drama of Harpers Ferry was played out in those narrow streets, along the tracks of the Baltimore and Ohio Railroad; and in the pounding waters of the gorge, cut between the mountains by the Potomac and the Shenandoah. To climb the mountain, to look down the wild precipices to the rivers and the village below, Thomas Jefferson once wrote, was worth a trip across the Atlantic . . .

The rivers are still the same, and the mountains and the brooding hills. There is no more beautiful, forgotten place in rural America than this corner where Virginia and Maryland and West Virginia meet. It is a country of blue mountains and mountain farms, of great golden hayfields and white-washed brick houses against the dreaming hills, and of steep, twisted roads cutting their way through banks of blood-red clay.

In the 1850's, Harpers Ferry was already an old town. Its surging water had made it an industrial center for over a hundred years. Now, in 1859, it produced annually about seven thousand muskets and three thousand rifles and small arms. In the big National Armory about two hundred thousand stand of arms were stacked and waiting. Naturally, the town was a prime military objective.

In the early morning hours of October 17, 1859, the telegraph wires crackled in the little town of Frederick, Maryland. An "insurrection" had broken out at Harpers Ferry. The eastbound express train had been fired on and halted, and the arsenal had fallen. Luther Simpson, baggagemaster of the train, had been held prisoner for an hour. He had seen the leader of the uprising, a middle-aged man, with gray hair and beard, called Bill Smith. He had heard him say to the conductor: "If you knew my heart and my history you would not blame me so much."

It was reported that most of the people in Harpers Ferry had fled. Mr. Simpson said: "I saw from five to six hundred Negroes, all having arms, and two or three hundred white men."

Richmond ordered out the regiment of "Greys." Three companies of artillery set out from Old Point Comfort, and a company of Marines from the Washington barracks. At the War Department in Washington there must have been shame, indeed. Every detail of the insurrection at Harpers Ferry had been outlined in an anonymous letter received at the Department during the summer. It had been ignored and destroyed.

Panic swept across the Southern states. For generations the South had lived under the fear of a slave insurrection, the tolling of the fire bell, which meant a rising of the slaves. Now — what dark terror walked the Virginia night? It was said that the Harpers Ferry bank had been robbed. It was said that the Armory had been taken and most of the surrounding countryside. Now and then a rifle crackled through the darkness. There was no other sound. Not a light was burning on the streets . . .

The citizens of Harpers Ferry were as much in the dark as the rest of the country. Among the raiders, several people had recognized "Bill Smith." He had rented a farm in the area several months earlier, and was well known at the Armory as an intelligent and useful kind of man, who had often dropped by for a visit to talk about his projected "mining operations."

Now, he and a group of followers were racing through the streets, shouting to the Negro slaves: "This will be a day that will long be remembered in the history of your race." The raiders tried to hand them pikes. "Did you never hear of John Brown . . .

old Osawatomie Brown?" the leader called to them. The slaves dropped the pikes and ran to hide under haystacks.

After twenty-four hours the raiding band was, at last, on the defensive. Earlier in the day they had taken prisoners from among the distinguished residents of the community, among them Colonel Lewis Washington. Before capturing them, the raiders had politely allowed them to eat breakfast. Then, as their promised reinforcements failed to arrive, and none of the slaves on the plantations outside came to seek their freedom, the raiders, their prisoners, and the prisoners' slaves retreated to the engine house of the Armory. One raider was captured. He began to talk. At 2:30 A.M. a telegraphic report seeped out of Harpers Ferry, more humiliating for the South than a disaster on the field of battle. The invading "army" was composed of seventeen white men and five Negroes!

A "beautiful clear autumn day" was dawning. Marching on Harpers Ferry was Colonel Robert E. Lee, Lieutenant J. E. B. Stuart, and a company of United States Marines.

The engine house in Harpers Ferry was a small, strong building of stone, with high-arched doors and windows and something of the look of a Gothic church. It had been under fire all night and, inside, the raiders had huddled in the dark, their prisoners to one side. The prisoners were never used as shields. The leader was to the front always. To Colonel Washington, he seemed the coolest, firmest man he had ever seen. One of his sons was already dead and another dying; the father placed one hand on the ebbing pulse, but clenched his gun firmly with the other. Through the night the dying boy kept crying; then the young voice faded . . . was still. The father called, but there was no answer. "I guess he is dead," the father said.

Through the night, the Virginia Volunteers stormed the building, but with no success. In the morning ninety Marines arrived at Harpers Ferry. Their leader, an armed man in civilian clothes, with graying hair and a dark mustache, stood on an elevation about forty feet from the Armory. Robert E. Lee "treated the affair as of no great consequence."

He despatched Stuart to parlay under a white flag. For him, the leader of the raiders opened the door about four inches, leaning his body against the crack. He would let the prisoners go, he said, if he and his men were given a safe escort out of town. It was with a start that Stuart recognized him as "old Osawatomie Brown, who had given us so much trouble in Kansas."

Now Lieutenant Israel Green ordered a fire engine used as a battering ram against the strong, double doors. They splintered and broke. Marines in blue with white belts stormed inside. Years afterward, Green still remembered his flashing glimpse of a lean man in a gray shirt with trousers tucked into his boots, kneeling on one knee with a gun in his hand, his "long, grey beard falling away from his face," and "looking quickly and keenly toward the danger that . . . had come upon him."

Only five or six of the raiding party were still alive, and this was "the only one left with some fight in him." Colonel Washington motioned toward him with his hand. "This is Osawatomie," he said. Green brought his saber down on Brown's neck.

Late in the day arrived Governor Henry Wise of Virginia. He was so ashamed, he said, that he would rather have had his arms and legs cut off than to face such a disgrace. To think of it — that twenty-two men should have captured "the government works and all Harpers Ferry, and have been able to retain them for one hour." Lee and his men had settled the matter in ten minutes. Even more incredible had been John Brown's capture of the prisoners, who protested that they were huddled in like a flock of sheep.

"Yes," said the bitter Governor, "you were in a corner and you were very much like sheep."

They asked John Brown why he had come. "I came to free the slaves," he said.

"You are mad and fanatical."

"And I think you people in the South are mad and fanatical. Is it sane to keep five million people in slavery . . . to murder all who would interfere with it?"

They asked him who had sent him there. "No man sent me here; it was my own prompting and that of my Maker . . . I acknowledge no master in human form."

They brought the Governor before him. Wise looked down at the man "cut and . . . bleeding and in bonds." He told the prisoner he had better prepare for death. Calmly, Brown retorted that the Governor would have a lot to answer for before God, and that he had better get ready, too. Amazed, Wise decided that this was no madman, but "the gamest man he ever saw," and the Southern press carried his words.

The hopes of years had gone up in the smoke of

Harpers Ferry. For two years now John Brown had dreamed of a fortress in the southern mountains. He had planned for a dozen different uprisings in a dozen different places at a single time, the slaves "to be taught to conquer their former homes." He wanted, as he had always said, to make slavery so unsafe as to render it unprofitable.

But even Brown admitted that the blow had been struck too soon. "It was by my own folly that I was taken," he said. He could have escaped and saved himself, but God was planning something for him ... all this was settled and decreed "millions of years before the world was made."

He begged to be excused from "the mockery of a trial," but was carried on a cot before Judge Richard Parker of the Circuit Court, tried, and found guilty on counts of insurrection, treason and conspiracy. The gulf between North and South was widening into an abyss of which no man could see the bottom. The Richmond *Enquirer* declared that Brown's raid had revived tenfold the idea of a Southern Confederacy; the New York *Herald* printed the news from Harpers Ferry alongside a speech by William Seward, forecasting the "irrepressible conflict." The North declared John Brown to be a saint. The South proclaimed him a devil.

On one point, all were agreed — North and South and Old John Brown himself: he must die. The South wanted him to die as a punishment and a warning; the North wanted him to die as a martyr. "Let no man pray that Brown be spared," said the Reverend Henry Ward Beecher. In far-off Concord, Henry Thoreau said: "Some eighteen hundred years ago Christ was crucified; this morning, perchance . . . the bravest and humanest man in all the country . . . was hung. His life could never do as much good as his death." As one magazine writer put it: "Old Brown — Osawatomie Brown . . . the Moses of the higher law" could never again "descend into the vulgar stagnation of common life." And John Brown bowed to God's will. "My object would be much nearer fullfillment if I should die," he said.

When the judge sentenced him to hang by the neck until he was dead, Brown sat solid as a stone. The court asked him if he had anything to say. To the people of the South he said: "Prepare yourself for a settlement of this question . . . You may dispose of me very easily. I am nearly disposed of now; but . . . this Negro question . . . the end of that is not yet." He said: "The United States will have to pay the penalty of her sin." He looked the judge in the eye. He spoke softly. He said: "I fought for the poor; and I say it was right, for they are as good as any of you." Then he went back to his cell to wait to die.

On the second of December, 1859, a bright, clear sun broke through the haze filming the Blue Ridge Mountains. By eight in the morning the air was ringing with the sound of hoofbeats, infantry, artillery, cavalry, the Petersburg Greys, horsemen in scarlet jackets.

The night before, workmen had completed the scaffolding. It stood on a hillock, one half mile from the jailhouse, a structure of stout uprights, some six feet from the ground and twelve feet wide, with a handrail built around the sides and down a flight of steps. From the crossbeam overhead hung a huge iron hook and a swinging rope.

This morning John Brown had written until ten thirty. He thanked the sheriff for his kindness to him, the mayor and the jailer who had had him in to supper the night before. He visited his "men" in their cells. One of them told him he was going to a better world.

"I know I am," John Brown said.

He stood, framed in the doorway of the jail, a lean man in black, his face radiant, his arms tied behind him. He walked out like a conqueror, his lips smiling. He climbed into a farm wagon and rode to his execution, sitting beside a black coffin and drawn by two white horses.

"You are more cheerful than I am, Captain Brown," said the undertaker, who was driving the wagon.

"Yes, I ought to be," John Brown said.

He looked around him. The cold air of December bit through his clothes. He looked up to the great wall of the Blue Ridge, flung against the horizon. Beyond the woods to the north, long strips of cloud wavered in the sky.

"This is a beautiful country," John Brown said. "I never had the pleasure of seeing it before."

"You are a game man, Captain," the undertaker burst out.

"Yes, I was so trained," John Brown answered. A few moments later he walked to his death with "unflinching firmness," as an onlooker, Thomas Jonathan "Stonewall" Jackson, later recorded.

Within a year Abraham Lincoln would be elected President of a divided country, and General Winfield Scott be called to mount cannon at either end of Pennsylvania Avenue for safety during his inauguration. Within a year South Carolina would leave the Union. Within a year and a month it was known that all the cotton states would go. Within sixteen months the gunfire would sputter across Fort Sumter; Robert E. Lee and J. E. B. Stuart and Thomas Jonathan Jackson would be joining the armies they were to lead.

In the North men repeated and remembered the words John Brown had scrawled out and handed to a prisoner a few moments before he died: "I, John Brown, am now quite certain that the crimes of this guilty land will never be purged away but with blood."

And the blood ran red across the battlefields of Shiloh and Chancellorsville, at Gettysburg and Antietam. John Brown's ghost would walk across the land and his voice would sound, asking over and over again all the unanswered questions. Out of the North, thousands of troops would march, singing his name. He would never rest; he would never die; he would pass into poetry and folklore and the smoke of burning campfires: "Weird John Brown," Herman Melville wrote, whose gray beard was the "meteor of the war."

But this was later. Now, against an empty cornfield in western Virginia, the skeleton of a scaffolding stood against the "dark and stormy" night sky.

Up from the South a bitter wind was blowing . . . John Brown was dead, the first martyr in that conflict in which the tall man from Illinois would be the last. In bleeding Kansas and at Harpers Ferry the fight for union had exploded into violence. Now the forty-year battle of words was over; and the long-drawn battle of swords and guns would begin.

And yet, in the end, it was words that would heal and reunite the broken country, the words spoken when the battles were finished. It was the blessed peace of words that would be remembered after the man who had spoken them was gone: "With malice toward none; with charity for all . . . let us . . . bind up the nation's wounds . . ."

In the end, the fight for union was won.

Index

Abolitionists, 76–77
Adams, John, 16, 35, 36, 99
Adams, John Quincy, 16, 34, 38–39, 48, 99
Alamo, 77–78
Austin, Stephen, 73

Baltimore and Ohio Railroad, 41–42, 121
Beecher, Reverend Henry Ward, 129
Benét, Stephen Vincent, 56
Benton, Thomas Hart, 31–32, 88, 98, 100
Bowie, Jim, 73
Brown, John, 118–20, 123, 125, 126, 127, 128–31, 132–33

Calhoun, John C., 9, 33–34, 38, 39, 46–52, 53, 56, 57, 58–59, 60–61, 63, 65, 66, 69, 70–71, 82–83, 88, 89, 93–95, 98, 100, 101, 107, 116
Calhoun, Patrick, 47
California, 89
Charleston *Mercury*, 96
Charlottesville, Va., 1
Cherokee Indians, 74–75
Clay, Henry, 16–19, 20–26, 27–33, 37, 38, 48, 56, 69, 83, 86–92, 98, 99, 100, 101, 102, 105
Co-lon-neh. *See* Houston, Sam
Compromise of 1850, 89–96, 98, 101, 106
Cowpens, Battle of, 47
Crockett, Davy, 73

Dartmouth College, 53
Davis, Jefferson, 88, 91
Douglas, Stephen A., 88, 89, 90, 109–11, 115, 117
Dred Scott decision, 107, 110

Emerson, Ralph Waldo, 97
Era of Good Feeling, 37

Faneuil Hall, 59, 97
Force Bill, 66, 69, 70
Fort Hill (Calhoun's home), 49–50
Fort Sumter, 132
Franklin, Benjamin, 4
Frederick, Md., 122
Fugitive Slave Law, 89, 106–7, 108

Giddings, Joshua, 106
Green, Lt. Israel, 126

Hamilton, Alexander, 4
Harpers Ferry, Va., 120–24, 125
Hayne, Robert Young, 57–59, 60
Healy, George, 59
Henry, Patrick, 4
Hermitage, 85
Houston, Sam, 65, 72, 73–75, 76, 77–82, 83, 84–85, 88, 89, 92, 99, 100, 101–3

Immigrants, 104–5
Indian Queen Inn, 62
Indians, 74–75, 82
Interposition. *See* Nullification

Jackson, Andrew, 38, 39–43, 48, 52, 62, 63–69, 71, 73, 75, 77, 79, 80, 82, 83, 84–85
Jackson, Rachel, 65
Jackson, Thomas Jonathan "Stonewall," 131, 132
Jefferson, Thomas, 1–6, 8–9, 11, 12–13, 25, 34–36, 51, 99, 121
Jefferson Day dinner, 62
Johnson, Gerald, 40

Kansas, 109, 120
Kansas-Nebraska Act, 109–10, 113, 114

Lawrence, Kan., 119
Lea, Margaret, 81
Lee, Colonel Robert E., 124, 125, 126, 132

134

Lincoln, Abraham, 14, 99, 111–16, 117, 131
Litchfield Law School, 48
Livingston, Edward, 64
Long Cane Massacre, 47
Louisiana, 51
Louisiana Purchase, 75

Madison, James, 51, 99
Manufacturing, U.S., 44
Marshfield, Mass., 53, 56
Maryland, 89
Mason-Dixon Line, 107
Massachusetts, 95, 106
Melville, Herman, 132
Mexico, 76
"Misery Debates," 19
Missouri, 2, 7, 15, 16, 17; debates, 15, 19, 20–23, 26
Missouri Compromise, 23, 26–28, 29, 34, 91, 107, 116
Monroe, James, 15–16, 33
Monticello, 2–4, 6, 34, 42

National Bank, 43
National Council of Cherokees, 75
New Hampshire, 54
New Mexico, 89
New York Herald, 128
New York Tribune, 107
Nullification, 51–52, 57, 62, 65, 68, 70, 71, 76

"Old Ironsides," 44
Omnibus Bill, 99

Paine, Thomas, 7
Parker, Judge Richard, 128
Parker, Reverend Theodore, 96
Personal Liberty Laws, 106
Phillips Academy, Exeter, N.H., 47–48
Pocahontas, 14
Polk, James Knox, 83
Pottawatomie Creek, 119

Randolph, John, 14–15, 21–22, 24–25, 28–29, 30–32, 38, 39

Raven, The. See Houston, Sam
Revere, Paul, 44
Richmond Enquirer, 128
Rivanna River, 1
Roberts, Jonathan, 22

San Jacinto, Battle of, 79
Saxe-Weimar, Duke of, 5
Schurz, Carl, 104, 105, 106
Scott, General Winfield, 66, 131
Seward, William H., 88, 120, 128
Simpson, Luther, 122
Slavery issue, 8–12, 15, 33, 76–77, 89, 100–101. See also Compromise of 1850
Smith, Bill, 122, 123
Smith, Dear, 73, 78
South Carolina, 64, 66, 70, 132
"South Carolina Exposition and Protest," 51
Stowe, Harriet Beecher, 108
Stuart, Lieutenant J. E. B., 124, 125–26, 132
Supreme Court, 106–7

Tallmadge, James, 8
Tariffs, 43–46; compromise, 69, 70
Texas, 72–73, 75–76; question of annexation of, 76, 80–81, 82–83; Republic recognized, 79
"Texas Revolution," 77–79
Thomas, Jesse B., 22, 23–24, 26
Thoreau, Henry, 129
Travis, W. Barrett, 77–78
Twin Sisters, 79
Tyler, John, 17, 69, 81, 83, 84

Uncle Tom's Cabin, 108
Underground Railway, 107–8
Utah, 89

Van Buren, Martin, 63, 79
Virginia, 42, 89; Old Dominion of, 11–12, University of, 1, 5

Washington, Colonel Lewis, 124, 125, 126

135

Washington, D.C., 25, 26
Washington, George, 9
Webster, Daniel, 6, 31, 34, 38, 39, 42, 47, 52–62, 68, 88, 90, 94, 95–97, 99, 100, 101, 102

Whittier, John Greenleaf, 96
Wilmot Proviso, 91
Wise, Governor Henry, 126–9

Yale University, 48